Bible 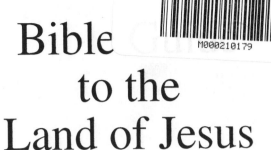 Guide
to the
Land of Jesus

Roy Turkington

Dedication

This book is lovingly dedicated to my wife Evelyn, and to my two children, Alistair and Andrea. As a family we traveled the length and breadth of Israel, Jordan and Egypt. Evelyn was a little more courageous than I in venturing into 'difficult' places - but we all went along for the ride! These adventures have created innumerable life-long memories that we will always cherish. And thanks to my mom and dad who, from my childhood, instilled in me the desire to travel.

TABLE OF CONTENTS

*"My young friend, we don't have
to prove the Bible; we have to
try and understand it!"*

Professor Benjamin Mazar

Source:
Machlin, Milt (1991). Joshua's Altar: the dig at Mt. Ebal.
William Morrow & Co., Inc. New York.

Arise, walk through the land

From August 1992 to June 1993 our family had the opportunity to live in Israel. I was on sabbatical from the University of British Columbia and used this time to foster new research links with colleagues at the Hebrew University of Jerusalem and the Ben Gurion University of the Negev. We rented an apartment in Bet Hakerem, about 3 km from the Old City of Jerusalem and about 7 km from Bethlehem. This became a very special year for us when we, as a family, spent most weekends exploring and visiting various parts of this country, and beyond - to Egypt and Jordan, and on a later visit, to Syria. It became our objective to follow God's commission to Abram, to "Arise, walk through the land in the length of it, and in the breadth of it" (Gen 13:17). We tried to visit the site of every recorded Bible event in Israel, provided there was some evidence that the site and location could still be identified with some degree of certainty - a number are rather tenuous - and a number are based on human invention rather than scriptural or archeological authority. Together we beat our way through bushes, drove through farmers' fields, along tracks rather than roads, through fruit groves, through shallow rivers, around military bases, into some quite dangerous areas, all to experience this land - and we only wish we had a book like this one to direct us to our locations. Such is the pace of development in Israel that maps become outdated notoriously quickly. Consequently, we often got lost, we needed directions, we were stoned, and we were robbed, but we just about met our objective as the book attests. It was never my objective to write a book. The book just happened as we accumulated information on the various places we visited. This book deals primarily with Israel, but as far as possible I have also provided relevant information for Egypt, Jordan and Syria. I have adhered fairly strictly to Bible sites even though these countries offer countless other natural and man-made treasures for visitors.

Even though this book is primarily about Bible locations in Israel, the country offers a lot more - history, geography, culture, and religions, for example. It is a long and narrow country, about 450 km from Metulla in the north on the border with Lebanon, to Eilat on the Gulf of Aqaba. At its widest it is only about 130 km. The country has some distinct regions. The southern third of Israel is an arid, but beautiful rocky desert - the Negev. A few mountain ranges more-or-less run the length of the country, separating the fertile coastal plain and Shepelah from the Jordan valley and Dead Sea (the lowest point on earth). The mountains of Galilee in the north are separated form the hill country of Judaea and Samaria (West Bank) in the center of the country by the Jezreel valley. So deserts, mountains, valleys, fertile fields, plains, forests, olive groves, and rocky outcrops may only be minutes apart.

Many travelers to the Holy Land are restricted to a predetermined tour schedule and tend to visit sites marked by impressive churches or ancient ruins. Few people visiting the Holy Land consider the more obscure Biblical sites as places of interest to visit. Yet, many places throughout the region can offer the visitor food for thought, meditation, and inspiration. Many of these towns and villages are off the beaten tourist track, nevertheless, they witnessed some of the most inspiring stories of the Old and New Testaments. There is a tremendous sense of history all around. Every hill and valley, town and village, seems to have some claim to fame. Bible stories take on a whole new dimension as they become real historical events that involved real people. It is exhilarating to follow the footsteps of Abraham, Moses, Joshua, and David, to sit where Solomon was crowned king, and to walk where Jesus walked. And if you are a serious traveler, take along with you a copy of Jerome Murphy-O'Connor's The Holy Land (Oxford University Press).

But a few words of caution. In spite of the natural beauty, and the friendliness of the people, access to many of the Bible sites may be difficult especially in the area variously known as "The West Bank", "Palestine", "Judaea and Samaria", "The

Occupied Territories", "The Administered Lands" etc. In many of these areas the people are intensely anti-Israeli, especially between Bethlehem and Hebron, and from Ramallah through Nablus to Jenin. Accessibility will vary according to the political and religious climate, and may be affected by curfews, strikes or even riots. Army road checks are often in place making some places out of bounds to travelers. While we took many risks we must obviously advise readers not to take such risks. Find out as much as you can about local conditions before traveling. Ask at tourist information offices or consult newspapers. Use your own personal discretion before you enter and, of course, you make these visits at your own risk. To reach many of these sites you will have to rent a car. You should be aware that your car rental insurance will not cover underbody car damage, or stoning!, so be careful where you bring your car. Having said all of this, you can generally move around quite easily and safely. It used to be a major problem to have yellow license plates when traveling in the West Bank - not any longer - although the green and white Palestinian plates may be advisable if tensions are high.

To use this book effectively you will also have to purchase a good Israeli Road Map; I recommend the Israel Touring Map, but any map that marks the main road route numbers is adequate. Also, a copy of Carta's Israel Road and Touring Guide is an excellent addition. Hand-drawn maps are provided near the end of the book to direct you to the general area of most of the sites. More detailed directions to the more-difficult-to-find sites are given at the end of the appropriate sections, indicated by the symbol ». While I have made every effort to be accurate in my directions, sometimes the trace of some of the dirt roads change, or may even be washed out. If your plans take you to more than about half a dozen National Park Sites, consider purchasing a pass when you visit your first site. With all this in mind, go out and enjoy this most fascinating region of the world.

Arise, walk through the land   v

MY FAVORITE SITES

Many sites throughout this region offer the visitor an opportunity for thought, meditation, and inspiration. Many have a strong Biblical and spiritual significance, others are inspirational because of their scenic value. I list here some of my own personal preferences; sites which in one way or another have made me pause for a longer look, or have caused me to ponder, or have enticed me back for more than one visit - your choices may differ.

Scenic
1. **En Avdat** (page 95): The view of En Avdat from the upper parking lot is one of the most breath-taking in Israel, perhaps only surpassed by #2 below.

2. **The Wilderness of Zin** (pages 94, 95): The wilderness of Zin as viewed from the Ben Gurion burial grounds beside the Sede Boqer campus of the Ben Gurion University of the Negev. Not only to you view an incredible landscape, but you see a segment of the route of the wilderness wanderings during the exodus.

3. **Petra** (page 138): How could any list not include a visit to Petra, arguably one of the most fascinating historical archeological sites on the earth.

4. **Elon Moreh** (page 44): This is located on Har Kabir. From the top you can see everywhere; the view is spectacular! To the north is Tirzah and Thebez; to the east the road follows a fertile plain and valley to the Jordan River; to the south is Mt. Gerezim, Nablus and Shechem; and to the west is Mt. Ebal - and if you know where you are looking you can see Joshua's altar.

5. **An awe-inspiring** flight over Jerusalem and surrounding areas using Kanfei air tours from Jerusalem airport.

Biblical history

1. **Jezreel** (page 111): This was the location of Naboth's vineyard, and where Queen Jezebel was killed. Outside of Jerusalem, this location is unparalleled in terms of the number of Biblical locations and events that are nearby. Within a short distance from west to east one can see (or almost see!) Megiddo, Valley of Armageddon, Ophrah (Gideon and his fleece), Nazareth, Mt. Tabor, Shunem, Mt. Moreh, the location of Gideon's battle against the Midianites, Gideon's spring and Mt. Gilboa (where Saul and Jonathan were killed).

2. **Mt. Gerezim** (page 44): The view from near the summit of Mt. Gerezim is awesome. From here you can see Mt. Ebal, todays Arab city of Nablus, the ruins of Biblical Shechem, Jacob's well, the tomb of Joseph, the village of Sychar (you can imagine the whole story unfold of Jesus and the woman at the well (Jn 4:1-26)), and the village of Elon Moreh nearby which God promised Abram that he would inherit the land.

3. **Beth Shemesh** (page 80): This site doesn't offer as much as the previous two, but it's still one of my favorites; this is Samson and Delilah country. You can see Zorah and Eshtaol, the Brook Sorek, and in the distance Tel Balatah which is Biblical Timnah. As you face west, stand and imagine the Ark of the God coming towards you from Timnah, on a cart being pulled by two cows.

4. **Jerusalem** (pages 1-25): Where to start? This is the Holy City (Is 52:1), the city of the great King (Mt 5:35), the city of truth (Zec 8:3). Every corner and every alley of the Old City, and of the region directly to the south of the Old City, seems to have some historical significance, much of it Biblical. Take this book and just start walking!

5. **Ai** (page 36): Few narratives in the Bible are described in as much detail as Joshua's second attempt to capture Ai (Jos 8). While standing on the ruins facing east down the valley

Arise, walk through the land   vii toward Jericho, you can easily see the whole story unfold - the route taken by the decoy group, the route taken by the actual ambush forces, where the ambush forces 'hid' and the ramp they used to invade the city, the ambush itself and the sacking of the city..... and so on.

6. **Altar of Manoah** (page 79): This is (or at least was) a rock altar as the Hebrews would have built an altar in the time of the judges. Many authorities believe that this could have been the altar where the angel of the Lord appeared to Manoah. However, the altar was moved, or dumped, during road construction and as of this time I don't know if it still exists - I couldn't find it in 1998.

7. **Gibeon** (pages 28, 29): The site itself is special and so is its surroundings. Here you can sit at the edge of a 23m deep cistern and envisage the battle between Joab and Abner's men at this very spot. Around you can see Ramah (the birthplace of the prophet Samuel), and of course, you are in the middle of the valley where Joshua prayed that the sun would stand still.

8. **Samaria** (pages 47, 48): It's almost worth the effort to go all of the way to the ruins at Samaria just to see the scant remains of the palace that belonged to Ahab and Jezebel. Besides the palace, the remaining ruins are worth seeing especially considering the centrality of this city to so many Bible events.

9. **Tel Dan** (page 130): A remarkable combination of Nature Reserve and Antiquity Site. One of the trails in the Reserve meanders through what seems like a thousand bubbling springs all contributing to the headwaters of the River Jordan. The Antiquity Site has the only eighteenth century BC mud gateway in the Middle East - dating to Canaanite times. Think about it - Abraham probably wandered through this gate 3800 years ago! The site also has a sacrificial altar, quite probably the one built by King Jeroboam.

10. **Elon Moreh and Joshua's Altar on Mt. Ebal** (pages 44, 45): Not easy ones to get to, but well worth the visit.

Meditation

1. **The Garden Tomb** (pages 8, 12): Now in the place where Jesus was crucified there was a garden; and in the garden was a new sepulcher, wherein was never man yet laid (Jn 19:41). Whether this is the tomb of Jesus or not, we don't know, but this is a quiet, contemplative spot in the middle of a noisy and busy East Jerusalem. This is one of the most special places in all of the Holy Land.

2. **Mt. Nebo** (page 144): This was God's appointed place for Moses to view the Promised Land. From Mt. Nebo, on a clear day, it seems you can see forever. Jericho is almost 20 km distant but it is only a fraction of the distance you can see north along the Jordan River valley and south along the Dead Sea. Straight across to the west, at a distance of over 40 km, you can clearly see the Russian Church of the Ascension atop the Mount of Olives.

3. **The Sea of Galilee** (pages 121-127): A short one-day tour around the Sea of Galilee offers the traveler access to many of the sites visited by Jesus during His ministry; the Mount of Beatitudes is particularly peaceful.

4. **Mt. Sinai** (page 135): This is one of the most venerated and important sites of the world's three great monotheistic religions - Judaism, Christianity and Islam. This is where God gave Moses the ten commandments and many other laws that still form the backbone of western ethics and morality. We don't even know for sure where the real Mount Sinai is located - but if you have the opportunity, visit the one in the southern Sinai anyway!

HOW TO LOCATE A SITE

We have to live with the fact that many Bible sites cannot be identified with certainty, and there are also a great many other sites which are not mentioned in the Bible. In addition, there is unfortunate 'competition' between various major denominations to display particular Christian sites. For example, in Jerusalem you will find at least two proposed sites for the Room of the Last Supper, Calvary, the tomb of Christ, the Ascension, and the martyrdom of Stephen, and there are at least four proposed prisons of Jesus. A number of these are insoluble at present and it is quite futile to try and sort them out.

This entire book has been designed to guide you through some of the confusion, to introduce you to the vast majority of the sites of the Holy Land, and to try to direct you effectively to each of them. Perhaps about one third of all sites are easy to find, are on the tourist-track and are marked on any decent map; I provide no directions on locating these sites - use a map and your tongue! However, many of the places are just a little bit more difficult to find, there are no sign posts, often the local citizenry won't know what you are talking about, and if they do, they may be totally bewildered why anyone should be interested in visiting this particular pile of historic rubble. In most cases the archeologists have long gone, digs have been either filled in (or perhaps fallen in), and the sites may not be that visually inspiring even though some grand archeological dig may have taken place in the past. For these sites, maps are provided at the back of the book to direct you to their general area. You should use these maps in conjunction with a good road map of Israel available from most bookstores. Then there are those sites that you haven't a dog's chance of finding without a lot of effort. Detailed directions to these more-difficult-to-find sites are given at the end of the individual sections, indicated by the symbol » and often accompanied by a map at the end of the book. Then there is a relatively small fourth group of sites that we searched for, but finally gave up. For most, we knew we were close, perhaps within a few hundred meters, but somehow couldn't quite stumble across any vestige of some past history; these few sites I indicate in the main text of the book. Then there are a few sites that were too inaccessible (e.g. Aroer on the Arnon gorge; Penuel in western Jordan). If you reach any of these, please let us know. Then there is a final group that I have not even listed. These may only be mentioned once in the entire scriptures and often in the book of Joshua where there are lists of cities as the land was divided up among the various tribes - at this point I estimated that the payoff wasn't worth the effort.

Finally, you will have to deal with the confusion of names. Because our maps use names that are English translations of Hebrew and Arabic words we can expect all sorts of spellings for the same place name - but if you sound them out phonetically, they will be similar. Many of the vowels seem to be interchangeable, and frequently you will see Q and K substituted, K and C, B and V, G and J, J and Y etc. Then there will be Hebrew names and Arabic names for the same place (e.g. Shechem and Nablus). Personally I have recorded six different signpost spellings for Bet Hakerem, or is it Beit Haccerem or is it ....? I sometimes use Tell (Arabic for mound) or Tel (Hebrew), Khirbet and Hurbat (Arabic and Hebrew respectively for ruins). And finally, the translators of the King James and the New International Version of the Bible, which are the two texts I have primarily used, will often use different spellings for place names. But don't let all of this discourage you, it's quite easy, and I hope I have provided just what you need to find out how to get to where you want to get to.

I have made every effort to be accurate in my directions, but sometimes the course of some of the dirt roads can be altered, or they may even be washed out - and of course, some archeologist may change his or her mind on the identify of a site! On all of the maps at the back of the book you will find either a distance scale, or else the actual number of kilometers between two points (marked by the asterisk [(]symbol). The markers below will help you interpret the maps:

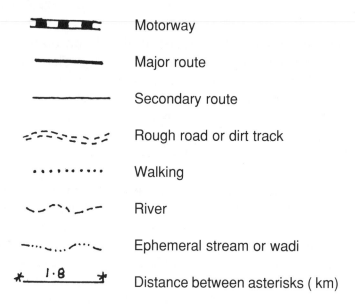

	Motorway
	Major route
	Secondary route
	Rough road or dirt track
	Walking
	River
	Ephemeral stream or wadi
	Distance between asterisks (km)

Acknowledgment:

I can't name, or even remember, all of the friends and acquaintances who helped us track down many of these sites, and who sometimes shared the experience with us. But especially I want to acknowledge and thank Linda, Deborah, Uriel, Nechama, Yoram, Avinoam and Musa.

"ARISE, WALK THROUGH THE LAND IN THE LENGTH OF IT, AND IN THE BREADTH OF IT"
Gen 13:17

IT IS A GOOD LAND

*"For the LORD thy God bringeth
thee into a good land, a land of brooks,
of water, of fountains and depths that
spring out of valleys and hills"*
Deut 8:7

IT IS A BEAUTIFUL LAND

*"It is a land of hills and valleys ..
a land which the LORD thy God
careth for; the eyes of the Lord
thy God are always upon it"*
Deut 11:11b,12a

IT IS GOD'S LAND

*"The land shall not be sold permanently,
for the land is Mine.."*
Lev 25:23

".. My land which I have given them"
2 Chr 7:20

"I brought you into .. My land"
Jer 2:7

".. they made My land their own possession"
Ezk 36:5

*"Oh Gog, I will bring you against My land,
so that the nations may know me
when I show myself holy."*
Ezk 38:16

*"..my inheritance, my people Israel,
for they scattered my people among
the nations and divided up my land."*
Joel 3:2

IT IS THE PROMISED LAND

*"..the LORD made a covenant with
Abram, saying, unto thy seed
have I given this land, from the
river of Egypt unto the Great
River, the river Euphrates"
Gen 15:18*

IT IS A HOLY LAND

*"And the LORD shall inherit Judah
his portion in the holy land"
Zec 2:12*

AN ABBREVIATED HISTORY
OF THE LAND

1950 BC	Abram arrived in Canaan
1350	Exodus from Egypt
1300 - 1250	Entry and conquest of the Promised Land
1200 - 1030	The period of the Judges
1030	Saul crowned as Israel's first king
1011 - 972	King David's reign
965 - 922	King Solomon's reign; first temple built
953 - 933	Division of the kingdom into Israel and Judah
721	Northern kingdom destroyed by the Assyrians
587	Jerusalem and the temple destroyed by Nebuchadnezzar The people of Judah exiled
537	Jews return from exile with Zerubbabel to rebuild the temple
520	Temple rebuilt
458	Return from exile with Ezra to teach the people
445 the	Return from exile with Nehemiah to rebuild walls of Jerusalem
332	Conquest of Palestine by Alexander the Great
332 - 168	Hellenistic Period
167	First Jewish revolt led by Judas Maccabees
64	Conquest of Palestine by Pompey
37 - 4	Reign of Herod the Great
4 BC - 1 AD	Birth of Jesus Christ
30 AD	Crucifixion of Jesus Christ
66 - 70	Zealots revolt against the Romans
73	The fall of Masada
132 - 135	The Bar Kochba revolt; crushed by Hadrian
395 - 638	The Byzantine period
638 - 1099	The Arab-Moslem period
1099 - 1291	The Crusader period

Arise, walk through the land

1250 - 1516	The Moslem Mameluke period
1516	Palestine conquered by the Turks
	Establishment of the Ottoman Empire
1536	Building of the present Old City walls of Jerusalem
1917	General Allenby conquers Palestine
	Balfour declaration
1922	British Mandate
1948	Proclamation of the State of Israel
	War of Independence
1956	Sinai campaign
1967	Six day war
1973	Yom Kippur war
1977	Egyptian President Sadat visited Israel
1979	Signing of peace treaty with Egypt
1993	Mutual recognition by Israel and the PLO
1994	Signing of peace treaty with Jordan

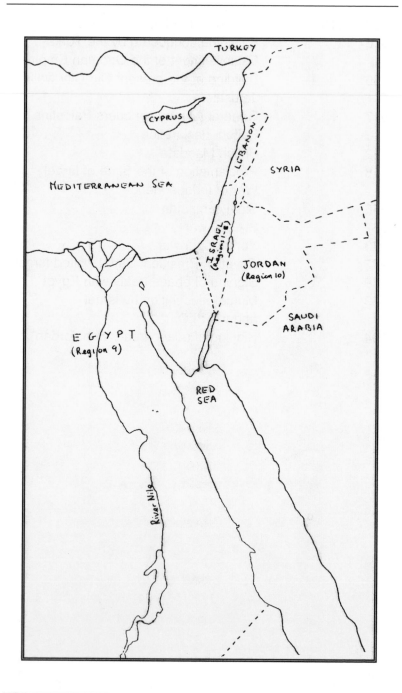

Arise, walk through the land

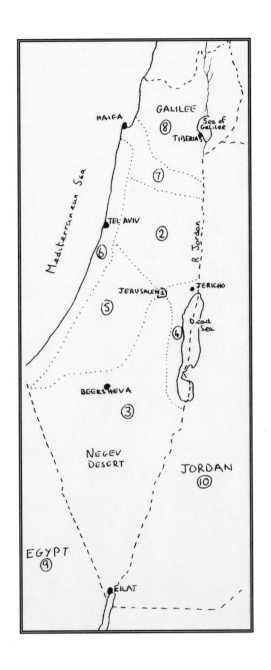

Arise, walk through the land

JERUSALEM

PRAY FOR THE PEACE OF JERUSALEM
(Ps 122:6)

Thus saith the LORD God; This is Jerusalem: I have set it in the midst of the nations and countries that are round about her. (Ezk 5:5)

Jerusalem, the city which the LORD had chosen out of all the tribes of Israel, to put his name there. (2 Chr 12:13)

The LORD had said, "My Name will remain in Jerusalem forever." (2 Chr 33:4)

Beautiful for situation, the joy of the whole earth, is Mount Zion .. the city of the great King. (Ps 48:2)

.. and Jerusalem shall be called a city of truth;.. (Zec 8:3)

The people of Jerusalem are strong, because the LORD Almighty is their God. (Zec 12:5)

On that day .. I will make Jerusalem an immovable rock for all the nations .. the LORD will shield those that live in Jerusalem ..and .. I will set out to destroy all the nations that attack Jerusalem. (Zec 12:3,8,9)

It will be inhabited; never again will it be destroyed. Jerusalem will be secure. (Zec 14:11)

O Jerusalem, the holy city (Is 52:1)

Jerusalem the holy city (Neh 11;1)

The city of the great King (Mt 5:35)

JERUSALEM

'possession of peace'
(Maps 1&2). Jerusalem, formerly Salem (Gen 14:18) and Jebus (1 Chr 11:4; Judg 19:10). Also called the City of David (1 Chr 11:7), Jerusalem is mentioned over 770 times in the Bible. The city has been destroyed seventeen times and rebuilt eighteen times. It was the capital of the ancient southern kingdom of Judah. The original City of David was on the spur of land immediately to the south of the Temple Mount area. It was first built on the hills bordered by two converging valleys, the Valley of Hinnom (Gehenna) to the west and south, and the Kidron Valley to the east. The Kidron Valley separates the Old City from the Mount of Olives. Today's Old City is about one kilometer square. The wall averages 12m high and has eight gates - seven open and one closed.

Gen 14:18	Melchizedek, King of (Jeru)Salem
Jos 15:8	Northern border of tribe of Judah
2 Sam 5:6-12	Conquest by David
2 Sam 24:18-25	David purchases Araunah's threshing floor
1 Ki 2:10	King David buried
1 Ki 6	Palace of Solomon
1 Ki 7:1-12	Religious and political capital of kingdom
2 Ki 25	Destruction by Nebuchadnezzar in 587 BC
1 Chr11:4-9	Political and religious capital of the kingdom
1 Chr 21:18-26	David purchased Araunah's threshing floor
Neh 3 & 6	Nehemiah rebuilt the walls
Ps 76:2	God's home
Ps 122:6	Pray for the peace of Jerusalem
Mt 27:11-26	Jesus on trial
Mt 27:31-50	Jesus crucified
Lk 24:1-12	Jesus rose from the dead
Acts 21:17	Paul arrived in Jerusalem
Acts 22:3	Paul was brought up in Jerusalem
Acts 22:30-23:11	Paul before the Sanhedrin

THE TEMPLE MOUNT (ARAB. HARAM ESH SHARIF)

(Maps 1 &2). The site of Biblical Mount Moriah ("The LORD will Provide" Gen 22:14), and of Araunah's threshing floor (2 Sam 24:18-25), 740m above sea level. It is referred to as the LORD's holy mountain (Is 27:13; 57:13; Ezk 20:40). The site is presently occupied by the Muslim Dome of the Rock (an ornamental shrine), and El Aqsa mosque. Originally the site of Solomon's, Zerubbabel's, and Herod's temples. Today, the most impressive feature from Herod's temple is the great temple 'platform' which is 490m long and 296m wide. The Western Wall (the Kotel), is part of the retaining wall built by Herod the Great ain 20BC to support the temple esplanade. The Samaritans believe that Mt. Gerezim near Nablus (Shechem) is the site of Biblical Mt. Moriah (but see 2 Chr 3:1).

Gen 22:2	God instructed Abraham to sacrifice Isaac
2 Sam 7:1-17	David wanted to build a house for God
1 Ki 5 & 6	Construction of Solomon's temple
1 Ki 8	Dedication of the temple
2 Ki 11:13-16	Murder of Queen Athaliah outside temple
2 Ki 12	King Joash repaired the temple
2 Ki 22	The book of the law found in the temple
2 Ki 25	Destruction by Nebuchadnezzar, 587 BC
2 Chr 3:1	Mount Moriah is in Jerusalem
Ezra 6:13-18	Rebuilding and dedication of the temple
Gospels	Many of Jesus' teachings
Mt 21:12-13	Jesus threw out the money changers
Mt 27:51	Veil of the temple torn in two
Mk 11:15-17	Jesus overturned money changers tables
Lk 1:5-25	The birth of John the Baptist foretold
Lk 2:22-38	Jesus presented at the temple
Lk 2:41-46	Jesus found in the temple
Jn 7:14-53	Jesus taught in the temple
Jn 8:2-11	The woman caught in adultery
Jn 8:48-59	Discussions with the Jews
Acts 3:1-10	Peter cured the lame man
Acts 3:11-26	Peter spoke to the people
Acts 5:12-16	Apostles spoke to the people

PINNACLE OF THE TEMPLE

Generally regarded as the top of the southeast corner of the wall of the temple mount from which there was a drop of some 45m to the Kidron Valley below. Some (very few) also consider the pinnacle to be the southwest corner of the wall.

Mt 4:5-7   The second temptation of Jesus
Lk 4:9-13   The third temptation of Jesus

THE BEAUTIFUL GATE

(Map 2).Sometimes also called the Golden Gate, it is in the eastern wall of the temple mount overlooking the Garden of Gethsemane and the Kidron Valley. It is assumed that the Eastern Gate of Herodian times is buried immediately below today's Beautiful Gate. This double gate is an early Byzantine structure and has been closed at least since Crusader times, some say in order to prevent the coming of the Messiah. This is traditionally the gate through which Jesus entered Jerusalem on Palm Sunday, and the one though which He will enter at His second coming.

Ezk 44:1-3   Messiah will enter Jerusalem
Acts 3:1-10   Peter healed the crippled beggar

BROAD WALL

(Map 1). This wall is about 7m wide (hence the name 'Broad Wall') and dated to the 8th century BC; it was originally about 8.5m high A section of the wall, also known as Hezekiah's wall, is exposed in the Jewish Quarter of the Old City. Hezekiah was preparing for the siege by Sennacherib's army and this is probably part of his "outer wall"

2 Chr 32:5   Hezekiah built an outside wall
Neh 3:8   Nehemiah repaired the city walls
Neh 12:38   Giving thanks for the repair of the wall

MIDDLE GATE

(Map 1). One of the towers (Israelite Tower) of this gate is exposed in the Jewish Quarter of the Old City, immediately adjacent to the Broad Wall.

Jer 39:3   Babylonians gathered after fall of Jerusalem

TREASURES OF THE TEMPLE

(Map 1). The Temple Institute is just around the corner from the Burnt House in the Jewish Quarter. A group of Jewish scholars and artisans are actively making priestly garments, implements, and vessels for the new, third, temple. The items are on display and include the High Priest's 24-carat gold crown, and robe, and many utensils including a 'mizrack' used to carry the blood for the sacrificial ceremony. Nearby it is worth visiting the Burnt House and the Herodian Residental Quarter.

HOUSE OR CHURCH OF ST. ANNAS

(Map 1). This is located inside the Convent of the Olive Tree in the Armenian Quarter of the Old City. Beside the church is an olive tree, which according to Armenian tradition, is an offshoot of the tree to which the Romans tied Jesus. Beside the tree, and built into the wall, is one of the stones that would have cried out if the disciples would not have praised God joyfully (Lk 19:40)!

Jn 18:12,13   Jesus brought to Annas
Jn 18:24   Annas sent Jesus to Caiaphas

CHURCH OF ST. MARK

(Map 1). A Syrian Orthodox church close to David Street in the Old City. Traditionally this is the site of the home of St. Mark's mother.

Acts 12:1-19   Peter escaped from prison and hid here

CATHEDRAL OF ST. JAMES

(Map 1). Located in the Armenian Quarter of the Old City, this is also believed to be the site of the beheading of James the half- brother of Jesus.

Acts 12:1,2   Disciple James, the brother of John beheaded

HEZEKIAH'S POOL

(Map 1) This is also called the Pool of Pillars, the Pool of the Patriarch's Bath (in Arabic Birkat Hammam el-Batrak). It is currently surrounded by buildings on all sides, is dry, and used as a rubbish dump. Josephus refers to it as Amygdalon, meaning 'almond tree'. It is given the name Hezekiah's pool because of a belief that this is the upper pool where King Hezekiah met messengers from the king of Assyria. There has been little archeological work but the pool probably dates to Herodian times. At that time it was fed by a conduit flowing from the Mamilla Pool which is now in Independence Pk. to the NW of the Old City. The conduit is still in existence.

2 Ki 18:17   King of Assyria's messengers met Hezekiah

» Just off Christian Quarter Rd. is the Street of the Copts (Aqabat Khan El-Aqbat). Walk, or climb, 50m along this street to the Coptic Khan on the left, a Coptic monastery dedicated to St. George. Go down the steps into the Khan and ask permission from some of the merchants to look through their back window! The little cobbler's store immediately opposite the entrance is a good bet. You can also get a limited view of the pool from the high view point in David's Citadel Museum inside the Jaffa gate.

CHURCH OF ST. JOHN THE BAPTIST

(Map 1) This Greek Orthodox church is the oldest in Jerusalem and the basement has some Byzantine remains. A silver icon in the church is said to be part of John the Baptist's skull. There is a tradition that this was the house of Zebedee, the father of James and John; there seems to have been some confusion between John the Baptist and John the Evangelist.

» You can see the silver dome of the church from the fountain in the Muristan. The entrance to the courtyard is from Christian Quarter Rd. As you walk down David St. (the Suq) turn on to Christian Quarter Rd. and pace about 30m. The entrance to the church is on the right and is recognized by having a painting of John the Baptist's head above the door!

CALVARY - GARDEN TOMB - CHURCH OF THE HOLY SEPULCHRE

(Map 1). Calvary (from Latin) and Golgotha (from Aramaic) both mean "the skull" or "the place of the skull." Two rival sites claim to be Calvary and claim to have Christ's tomb. First is the Church of the Holy Sepulchre located in the Christian Quarter of the Old City. In the early 4th century this site was occupied by a temple dedicated to Venus - a scandal to Christians because of its sexual implications and practices of prostitution. Such was the disgust by the Christian community that Bishop Macarius convinced the Roman Emperor Constantine that the tomb of Christ was beneath the Temple. With Constantine's permission the temple was destroyed and the first Church of the Holy Sepulchre was constructed. Some remains of the 4th century church and the earlier temple can be seen inside St. Alexander's Church and inside the store room of Zalatimo's Sweet Shop. The second proposed site, Skull Hill, was advocated by British General Charles Gordon in 1885, and is about 230m from the Damascus Gate. Skull Hill, often called Gordon's Calvary, was reduced to its present shape by quarrying, mostly during Solomonic times for the building of the temple. Skull Hill, in some form, was present at the time of Christ and the flat area below it, now occupied by the Arab Central Bus Station, was an execution place in Roman times. Gordon's Calvary has been widely adopted by Protestants while the site at the Church of the Holy Sepulchre is accepted by the Roman Catholic and Orthodox faiths*.

Mt 27:32-28:7
Mk 15:21-16:8

Lk 23:34-24:12
Jn 19:17-20:18
Heb 13:12
A third site has recently been proposed to be located on the Mount of Olives. This proposal depends on an interpretation of Mt 27:51, 54; Mk 15:38, 39; Lk 23:45, 47 that the centurion present at the crucifixion also observed the tearing of the Temple curtain - which could only be done from the Mt. of Olives. This is generally regarded as a weak argument.

SAINT ALEXANDER'S CHURCH, AND ZALATIMO'S SWEETS

(Map 1). Inside the church, and in the store room of the shop, are some remains of the original 4th century Church of the Holy Sepulchre and of the earlier temple. The church also has part of Hadrian's Arch, some Herodian walls and pavement, and the "eye of the needle" *(Mt 19:24).*

» *St. Alexander's Church is located just east of the Church of the Holy Sepulchre. Zalatimo's Sweets is located where the stairs to the 9th Station of the Cross leaves from Suq Khan ez-Zeit St. Give the store owner a few shekels, or purchase a pastry, and ask him to let you visit his storeroom. After you have maneuvered a few crates of Coca Cola and other obstacles you will see a few scant ruins of the former buildings.*

PRAETORIUM

(Map 1). This was a place known as the Lithostratos or Stone Pavement (Gabbatha in Aramaic; Jn 19:13) and was Pilate's judgment hall. It was assumed to be in the Antonio Fortress which was the residence of the Roman procurators. One traditional location of this site is in the Ecce Homo Convent of the Sisters of Zion at the beginning of the Via Dolorosa. However, most scholars either argue that this site is not old enough or is in the wrong location. Some scholars place the Lithostratos in El-Omariyeh College (see Via Dolorosa below), and others in Herod's Palace, a site now occupied by David's Citadel beside Jaffa Gate.

Mt 27:27-31   Jesus given a purple robe and crown of

thorns
Mk 15:16-20   Jesus given a purple robe and crown of
thorns
Acts 21:31   A Roman garrison housed here

ECCE HOMO ARCH
(Map 1). The reconstructed ruins of this arch are now part of the church inside the Ecce Homo Convent of the Sisters of Zion and the beginning of the Via Dolorosa. Ecce Home is Latin for 'Behold the Man'.
Jn 19:1-5   Pilate presented Jesus to the mob

PRISON OF CHRIST
(Map 1). Next door, to the west, of the Ecce Homo Convent, is a Greek Orthodox Church which claims to have the prison of Christ and of Barabbas. There are additional prisons of Christ inside the Church of the Holy Sepulchre, the Church of St. Peter in Gallicantu and at the Armenian house of Caiaphas just outside Zion gate.
Mt 27:15-26   The release of Jesus or Barabbas
                Also: Mk 15:6-15; Lk 23:13-25; Jn 18:39-40

VIA DOLOROSA ETC.
Christ's traditional journey to Calvary. The route begins inside the El-Omariyeh College just east of the Ecce Home arch. It winds through the Muslim and Christian Quarters of the Old City ending at the 14th Station of the Cross inside of the Church of the Holy Sepulchre. Notably, this route is not marked on the sixth century Medeba map, and the route is based on faith rather than history.
Mt 27:27-33; Mk 15:1-20
Lk 22:54-23:33; Jn 18:12-19:17

Just to the east of the Praetorium, and up an alleyway to the left, you will find the Prison of Peter. Further along, just beyond the Pool of Bethesda and before the Lion's Gate you will find a door marked "Birthplace of the Virgin Mary" Neither location is supported by any historical evidence.

POOL OF BETHESDA
'house of grace'
(Map 1). Today this pool is inside the grounds of the Crusader Church of St. Anne. In Byzantine tradition, the church is built on the site of the home of the virgin Mary and her parents Joachim and Anne. There is a grotto (crypt) beneath the church where Mary was supposed to be born.
Jn 5:1-15   The healing of the paralytic man

SOLOMON'S, OR ZEDEKIAH'S QUARRIES
The entrance to Solomon's Quarries is at the base of a rocky cliff under the northern wall of the Old City, 100m east of Damascus gate, and immediately opposite Gordon's Calvary. Tradition says that King Zedekiah hid here as he fled from the Babylonians. The quarry was used as a source of stone for the temple building projects by King Solomon and by King Herod the Great.
1 Ki 6:7   Stone dressed for Solomon's temple
1 Ki 5:15-18   Solomon's stone workers for the temple

JEREMIAH'S GROTTO
Is it nothing to you, all you who pass by? Look around and see. Is any suffering like my suffering that was inflicted on me, that the Lord brought on me in the day of his fierce anger? Lam 1:12

In Jewish tradition this is the place where Jeremiah wrote the book of Lamentations. The grotto is a cave at the eastern end in the hill of Calvary, blocked from view by a Muslim mosque and an Arab bus station. Jeremiah describes the scenes enacted (Christ's crucifixion) only a few meters away nearly 600 years afterward (Lam 1:12-16).
Jer 38:6   Jeremiah imprisoned in a cistern

THE GARDEN

Beside the site of Gordon's Calvary is a garden with a tomb (see book cover photograph) dating from Roman times, and believed by many to be the garden and tomb of Joseph of Arimathea. The tomb had a rolling stone mechanism.

Jn 19:41   Where Jesus was crucified there was a garden

» The Garden Tomb is about 150m north of Damascus gate along the Nablus Rd.

CORNER STONE OF THE THIRD TEMPLE

»As you leave the Garden Tomb and enter Nablus Rd., turn right. Walk about 150m uphill to the intersection where there is a turning circle in front of a gas station. The cornerstone for the third temple is situated in the middle of the turning circle. Unfortunately, the location of this stone keeps changing so it may not be in this location by the time this book is printed! You may find the current location of the stone by phoning a local group of Jews called The Temple Mount Faithful.

STEPHEN'S MARTYRDOM

(Map 2). Two sites lay claim to the location of the martyrdom of Stephen. One, and probably the most authentic, is that Stephen was martyred at the base of skull hill at the site of today's Arab bus station in East Jerusalem. This was a traditional place of execution in Roman times and is close to Damascus gate (formerly known as Stephen's gate). Immediately north of the Garden Tomb on Nablus Rd. is the compound of the French Dominican Fathers. On the grounds of the monastery is the Church of St. Etienne (St. Stephen) and Ecole Biblique et Archeologique Francaise. In the fifth century a church was built here to house relics of Stephen. A second site is the Greek Orthodox Church of St. Stephen just across from the Garden of Gethsemane and close to the Lion's, or St. Stephen's, Gate. You can visit the Church of St. Etienne by ringing the doorbell on the gate of the compound,

and asking for someone to open; they are generally very friendly. The Orthodox Church of St. Stephen is another matter; and I have never known the church to be open - but according to some travel guides it occasionally is so.

Acts 7:54-60   Stephen stoned to death

TOMBS OF THE KINGS

This is not a Bible site but is of Biblical interest. At one time these were thought to be the tombs of the kings of Judah. This claim has long been abandoned because the tombs are too young and they are not inside the city wall of that time (see Royal Tombs entry).

» Continue along Nablus Rd. beyond the Church of St. Etienne for about 1 km to near the junction with Saladin St. The tombs are just a few meters south of the American Colony hotel.

NOB

In Benjamin (Neh 11:32)

A town northeast of, and apparently within sight of, the Holy City. Some identify the site as today's Sha'fat about 3 km north of Jerusalem on the road to Ramallah, and others close to the site of today's Mount Scopus Campus of the Hebrew University at the northern end of the Mount of Olives.

1 Sam 21:1-9   David ate the consecrated bread
1 Sam 21:2   David given refuge as he fled from Saul
1 Sam 22:17-19   Saul ordered Doeg to kill 85 priests
Neh 11:32   Settled by Benjaminites after the captivity
Is 10:32   Assyrian army camped within sight of the
                 Holy City

MADMENAH

As for Nob in the previous entry, Madmenah was supposed to be in the locality of Sha'fat.

Is 10:31　　　　　On the route of the invading Assyrian army

MOUNT OF OLIVES

The mountain on the east side of Jerusalem (Ezk 11:23, Zec 14:4) at 817m above sea level. Also called Olivet (Acts 1:12), it is a Sabbath day's journey from Jerusalem (Acts 1:9-12). The prophets Haggai, Zechariah and Malachi are buried near the summit. Their tombs are located about 50m north of the main viewpoint over the Old City at the top of the path/road that leads down to the garden of Gethsemane and the Kidron Valley. The Mount Scopus Campus of the Hebrew University of Jerusalem is situated on the northern part of the Mount of Olives.

Num 19:1-22　　　Sacrifice of the red heifer
2 Sam 15:30-32　David fled from Absalom
1 Ki 11:7-8　　　Solomon built altars for pagan gods
2 Ki 23:12-13　　Josiah destroyed pagan altars
Zec 14:3-4　　　Mount of Olives will cleave in the middle
Mt 21:1-10　　　The Messiah enters Jerusalem
Mt 24:3　　　　　Jesus taught about signs of end times
Mt 26:30　　　　　After the Lord's supper
Mk 13:3,4　　　　Jesus taught about end times
Mk 14:26　　　　　After the Lord's supper

Mosque of the Ascension and Russian Church of the Ascension.

Luke 24:50,51 records that Jesus went back to heaven from the vicinity of Bethany.

Lk 24:51　　　　　The ascension of Jesus
Acts 1:9-12　　　The ascension of Jesus

»There are two proposed locations - the Muslim mosque which is nearly always open, and the Russian church which is nearly always closed. The mosque displays what they claim to be Jesus' footprints! The entrance to the Russian church is about 150m north of the

mosque along the main road. Look for a large green gate up a slightly inconspicuous alleyway. Make an effort to get in because they have beautiful grounds.

Church of the Pater Noster (Eleona Church, or the Grotto of the Teaching).

The traditional site where Jesus foretold the destruction of Jerusalem (Mk 13:1-4). Claims are made that this is where Jesus taught the disciples 'The Lord's Prayer'. Lk 11:1-4 may have been taught here but Mt 6:5-15 was taught at the Mt. of Beatitudes in Galilee. The church has the Lord's Prayer in 104 languages presented on beautifully colored ceramic tile.

Mt 24 & 25   The Olivet discourse
Lk 21:37; Jn 8:1 Jesus' 'home' on the Mt. of Olives
Jn 3:1-15   Jesus taught Nicodemus

Church of Dominus Flevit
Lk 19:41   Jesus wept over Jerusalem

Church of Mary Magdalene
» As you enter the gates of the Church of Mary Magdalene, the main steps climb up to the right. Don't go that way! Rather, turn left along a narrow path for about 30m and you will come to about five ancient rock-cut steps which originally led to the top of the Mount of Olives. This may have been the route taken by the priests for the sacrifice of the red heifer (Num 19:1-22).

GETHSEMANE
'olive press'
(Map 2). A garden (olive grove [Jn 18:1]) at the bottom of the Mount of Olives, across the Kidron Valley and opposite the temple mount (Mk 13:3; Jn 18:1). Today the site is shared by various denominations. The main site is the Church of All Nations (also called the Church of the Agony). Immediately adjacent is the Grotto of Gethsemane, the site of Christ's betrayal and arrest, and probably one of the most authentic of all Christian sites (Lk 22:41). Uphill is the Russian site where

they have the Church of Mary Magdalene. And close by is the Church of the Assumption (see Dormition Abbey entry) which claims to be the site of Mary's assumption to heaven, and to have her tomb as well as the tombs of her parents Anne and Joachim. The Bible is silent on the death and burial of Mary.

Mt 26:36-45   Jesus prayed and the disciples slept.
                     Also: Mk 14:32-41; Lk 22:39-46
Mt 26:46-55   Jesus arrested
                     Also: Mk 14:42-50; Lk 22:47-54; Jn 18:1-12

KIDRON VALLEY-VALLEY OF JEHOSHAPHAT

(Map 2). Also called the Brook of Cedron. The Valley of Jehoshaphat ('Jehovah is judge'), also called the valley of decision (Joel 3:2), is that part of the Kidron Valley that separates Jerusalem and the temple mount from the Mt. of Olives to the east. The Kidron Valley runs to the south then to the east through the Judean wilderness where it enters the Dead Sea just south of Qumran.

1 Ki 15:13   King Asa burned grandmother's Asherah pole (also 2 Chr 15:16)
2 Ki 23:4,12   Josiah ordered destruction of pagan idols
2 Ki 23:6   Common cemetery of Jerusalem
Neh 2:13-15   Nehemiah inspected the walls at night
Jer 31:40   The valley will become holy to Jehovah
Joel 3:2,12   The Lord will judge nations in the valley

Absalom's Pillar

(Map 2). Situated in the Kidron Valley but not Absalom's tomb. This structure is dated to the first century AD. Immediately behind it is the Tomb of Jehoshaphat.

2 Sam 18:18   Absalom built a monument

Zechariah's Monument and Bnei Hezir Tomb

(Map 2). These are immediately adjacent and to the south of Absalom's pillar. The name of the monument may refer to Zacharias, father of John the Baptist. A tunnel leads from the Monument to the Tomb. Part of the inscription over the Tomb

refers to the priestly family of Hezir.

1 Chr 24:15   Priestly family of Hezir; held the 17th watch

Shebna's tomb
About 100m south of Zechariah's monument in the Arab village of Silwan, is the tomb of Pharaoh's daughter and about 60m beyond this is a tomb belonging to "the Royal Steward", Shebna, who was in charge of King Hezekiah's palace. A person's place of burial was considered very important and Shebna coveted a tomb worthy of a king. I have not personally visited Shebna's tomb (but believe me, I have tried extremely hard to find it!) so you will have to ask for specific directions.

Is 22:15-19   Shebna cut his tomb (in Silwan)
Is 36:3   Shebna demoted to secretary

CITY OF DAVID
(Map 2). King David captured the Jebusite city of Jebus and it became the City of David (or the City of Judah [2 Chr 25:28]). It occupied the spur of land immediately to the south of the Temple Mount area and overlooks the Kidron valley to the east. Parts of the original Jebusite wall and of David's additions are visible just downhill from Warren's shaft. The following five sites are all associated with the City of David: The stepped-stone structure, Gihon spring, Hezekiah's tunnel, Pool of Siloam, and the Royal tombs. While no remains of King David's palace have been uncovered it was probably high on the hill. From this vantage, either looking downhill, or across to Silwan, it is easy to visualize how David saw Bathsheba bathing (2 Sam 11:2).

1 Chr 11:4-9   David captured Jerusalem

THE STEPPED-STONE STRUCTURE
(Map 2). Various archeologists have tried to identify the stepped-stone structure which is visible in the 'Area G' excavation site in the City of David. Some have suggested that it is the "Fortress of Zion" (2 Sam 5:7). More commonly it is associated with the Biblical millo which was probably a

---

Arise, walk through the land   17

supporting wall, or perhaps a tower

2 Sam 5:9	David built in this area
1 Ki 9:15	Solomon uses forced labour for building
1Ki 9:24	Solomon built the millo
2 Ki 12:20	King Joash killed in the house in the millo
1 Chr 11:8	David fortified this area
2 Chr 32:5	King Hezekiah reinforced the millo

Other excavations beside the stepped-stone structure uncovered a seal 'factory'. One of the seals found was that of Gemariah the son of Shaphan.

Jer 36:10,11	Baruch read from the Word of the Lord
Jer 39:8; 52:13	Nebuchadnezzar burned Royal Palaces

GIHON SPRING

(Map 2). From earliest times this is the only continuous source of fresh water near Jerusalem; today it is commonly called the Virgin's Fountain. It discharges fifty cubic meters of water per hour into Hezekiah's Tunnel. The shaft (called Warren's shaft) by which Joab infiltrated the Jebusite city can be reached from Gihon spring and Hezekiah's tunnel.

2 Sam 5:6-8	Jebusite city captured by David's forces
1 Ki 1:28-45	Solomon anointed king of Israel
1 Chr 11:6	Joab infiltrated the city
2 Chr 32:30	King Hezekiah blocked the spring

HEZEKIAH'S TUNNEL

(Map 2). This tunnel, also called Siloam tunnel (not to be confused with the Siloam channel) was built in 701 BC in anticipation of a siege by King Sennacherib of Assyria. The tunnel drops only 35cm (other sources cite anything up to 2.1m; <1/2% grade) over its 533m (1748') length. It averages 1.75m high, and flows from the Gihon spring to the Pool of Siloam. It takes approximately 45 mins to wade waist-deep through the length of the tunnel beginning at the Gihon Spring. Bring a good flash light, clothes and footwear that you don't mind getting wet - and do it on a hot day so that you can

drip-dry at the Pool of Siloam! If you are the slightest bit claustrophobic don't even think of trying this even though it is an easy walk, you have no chance of getting lost, and it is exciting. There is usually an endless supply of Arab lads at the Gihon Spring who will guide you through the tunnel for a negotiable fee - it's worth it!

2 Ki 20:20   King Hezekiah built a tunnel
2 Chr 32:30   King Hezekiah built a tunnel

POOL OF SILOAM

(Map 2). Originally built by King Hezekiah shortly before 700 BC. Noted scholar R.A. Stewart Macalister, referring to the hymn 'By cool Siloam's shady rill how sweet the lily grows', says, "In the whole vast range of English literature there is probably not to be found another sequence of ten words containing a greater number of inaccuracies." Also written as Siloah and Shiloah.

2 Ki 20:20   King Hezekiah built the pool
Neh 3:15   Nehemiah repaired the walls of the pool
Is 8:6   Siloam (called Shiloah) and Euphrates
Is 22:9   Oracle against the city
Jn 9:6-11   Cure of the man born blind

ROYAL TOMBS

(Map 2). First temple period tombs have been excavated in the southern end of the City of David about 60m northeast of the Pool of Siloam. These may have been the royal tombs of King David and other kings of Judah although this claim is disputed by many. The royal tombs were evidently in the City of David, and perhaps in the palace garden, the garden of Uzza (2 Ki 21:18,26). The Pool of Siloam was "by the King's garden" (Neh 3:15) and apparently not too far from the tomb of David (Neh 3:16). In 2 Chr 32:33 King Hezekiah is said to have been buried "on the hill where the tombs of David's descendants are." The burial of later kings (Manasseh, Josiah, Amon, and Jehoiakim) is noted, but never located in the City of David. A burial complex has been located inside the grounds of the

Church of St. Etienne. Their style indicates they belonged to wealthy and important people and have lead some to suggest that this may be the burial place of later kings of Judah, from the time of Manasseh.

1 Ki 2:10	King David buried
1 Ki 11:41-43	King Solomon buried
1 Ki 14:31	King Rehoboam buried
1 Ki 15:8	King Abijam (Abijah, 2 Chr 14:1) buried
1 Ki 15:24	King Asa buried
1 Ki 22:50	King Jehoshaphat buried
2 Ki 8:24	King Jehoram (Joram) buried (but see 2 Chr 21:20)
2 Ki 9:28	King Ahaziah buried
2 Ki 12:21	King Joash buried (but see 2 Chr 24:25)
2 Ki 14:20	King Amaziah buried (City of Judah, 2 Chr 25:28)
2 Ki 15:7	King Azariah buried
2 Chr 26:23	King Uzziah buried
2 Ki 15:38	King Jotham buried
2 Ki 16:20	King Ahaz buried (but see 2 Chr 28:27)

SILOAM

The village of Silwan lies on the slopes of the south part of the Mount of Olives directly opposite the City of David. The Arab name Silwan is a corruption of the New Testament name Siloam, which in turn is a corruption of the Hebrew name Shiloah.

Lk 13:1-5   Tower fell on 18 people

» From the 'Royal Tombs' walk east for a few meters to the edge of the escarpment and look over the edge. The base of a large defensive tower may be seen. This is not necessarily the tower of Siloam but it reminds us of the story that Jesus told.

HINNOM VALLEY - HELL

(Map 2). In Hebrew, Gai Ben Hinnom (the Valley of the son of Hinnom - Jer 7:32; 19:5,6), is designated as Topheth (2 Ki 23:10; Jer 7:31), the Valley of Slaughter (Jer 7:31-34) or simply as the valley of Hinnom (Neh 11:30). Rubbish from Jerusalem was burned here, and it was also used as a place where parents sacrificed their children to pagan gods (Chemosh and Molech [1 Ki 11:7; 2 Ki 23:13; Jer 7:31]). From the abbreviated name 'Valley of Hinnom', Hebrew ge'hinnom, came the Greek 'gehenna' consistently translated in the New Testament as 'hell'.

2 Ki 23:10   Children sacrificed to Molech
2 Chr 28:1-4   Ahaz king of Judah sacrificed his sons
2 Chr 33:6   Manasseh king of Judah sacrificed his sons
Is 30:33   A fire pit (probably for child sacrifices)
Jer 7:31   Children sacrificed in fire

» The valley is west and south of the Old City of Jerusalem.

AKELDAMA AND TOMB OF ANNAS

(Map 2). A corruption of the Hebrew aker dam, literally meaning Field of Blood. The Greek Orthodox monastery of St. Onuphrius today occupies much of the area known as Akeldama. Although referred to as the Field of Blood or the Potter's Field, it is unlikely that this was a graveyard for only the poor or for strangers because there are so many finely decorated burial caves. One of the tombs may be that of Annas, the High priest (Lk 3:2; Jn 18:24; Acts 4:6), and father-in-law of Caiaphas the high priest (Jn 18:12-13). A chapel in the monastery, called the Refuge of the Apostles, is in a cave which tradition identifies as the place where the apostles fled after Jesus' arrest (Mk 14:43-50).

Jer 18:1-4   Jeremiah at the potter's house
Mt 27:7-10   Priests bought Potter's field (Zec 11:12,13)
Acts 1:18, 19 Judas Iscariot died in the field of blood

» The Greek Orthodox monastery is located on the southwest corner of the junction of the Hinnom and Kidron valleys. The monastery is

not generally open to the public but if you go up to the metal door, put your hand through, and push the red button, you will probably get a response. The resident monk is extremely friendly, knowledgeable and chatty; or you can try making arrangements through the Christian Information Center just inside Jaffa gate. The presumed tomb of Annas the High Priest is situated east of the monastery about midway between the monastery and the road. It has the remains of the entrance, and the ceiling is finely decorated - but you may have to excuse the Bedouins and their goats before you enter!

EN ROGEL
'fuller's well'
(Map 2). A 38m-deep well in the Kidron Valley near the junction with the Hinnom Valley, on the border of Benjamin and Judah (Jos 15:7). Also referred to as Job's Well, or Bir-Ayyub, and it may be the Jackal Well (NIV) or dragon well (King James) in Neh 2:13.

2 Sam 17:17-22 Jonathan and Ahimaaz stayed here
1 Ki 1:9   Adonijah sacrificed sheep
Neh 2:13   Nehemiah inspected the wall

» From the tomb of Annas, go downhill into the village for about 100m to a very small mosque with a tiny green dome. In a garden attached to the east of the mosque, you will find the well covered with two painted blue grills. If you ask for directions, ask for Bir-Ayyub, because it is the only name the local people recognize.

MOUNT OF OFFENSE
Also called 'The mount of corruption', this hill is situated above the village of Silwan opposite the convergence of the Kidron and Hinnom valleys.

1 Ki 11:5-7   Solomon built pagan altars
2 Ki 23:13   Josiah pulled down Solomon's altars

KETEF HINNOM
In Hebrew, "The Shoulder of Hinnom". The hill on which St. Andrew's Scottish Church is built is on the watershed between the Hinnom and Rephaim Valleys (see Baca Valley). It rises to

almost 750m above sea level, or 80m above the Hinnom. The oldest known fragment of a Bible text was found in a burial cave close to the courtyard of the church. *This fragment contains the Priestly Benediction (Num 6:22-27) incised on a silver plaque and is dated from late 7th century to early 6th century BC. The fragment is on display at the Israel Museum, Jerusalem.*

Num 6:22-27	"The LORD bless thee and keep thee..."
Jos 15:8	The border between Judah and Benjamin
Jos 18:16	The border between Judah and Benjamin

» Climb the first set of steps up into the church, to the platform. Look out over the wall and the open cave is directly below you. Notice the flat covering to the cave which has more than six "head rests" for holding bodies.

MOUNT ZION

*"Beautiful for situation, the joy of the whole earth,
is mount Zion, on the sides of the north,
the city of the great King" Ps 48:2*

*By the rivers of Babylon we sat and wept when
we remembered Zion.* *There on the poplars
we hung our harps, for there our captors asked
us for songs, our tormentors demanded
songs of joy; they said, "Sing us one
of the songs of Zion!" Ps 137:1-3*

This was the lower eastern hill of Jerusalem known as Ophel (2 Chr 27:3, 33:14; Is 32:14) or the City of David. Often used in connection with rejoicing and strength (Ps 48:11; 74:2; 76:68; 125:1; Is 8:18) and deliverance (Joel 2:32; Obad 1:17). Later when Mt. Moriah became the temple hill and the ark of the covenant brought to the temple, the name was transferred (2 Chr 5:2). The name currently refers to the western hill of the upper city where we find the traditional King David's tomb, the House of Caiaphas, the Room of the Last Supper, and the Dormition Abbey - and the grave of Oskar Schindler. *The*

Dormition abbey apparently marks the location of Mary's assumption to heaven although this claim is challenged by the Church of the Assumption beside Gethsemane.

2 Sam 5:7	City of David fortress of Zion
2 Sam 6:10-12	The Ark of God in the citadel of David
2 Chr 33:14	King Manasseh rebuilt the wall
Is 2:3	The mountain of the Lord
Is 8:18	Jehovah dwells on Mt. Zion
Is 18:7	The place of the name of the Lord of hosts
Is 24:23	The Lord of hosts shall reign in mount Zion

SAINT PETER IN GALLICANTU

Traditionally this is the place where Jesus appeared before Caiaphas (meaning 'a searcher') and where Peter denied the Lord. It contains a so-called prison of Christ. The authentic House of Caiaphas is probably about 200m to the north in the Armenian church immediately outside Zion Gate.

Mt 26:57-67	Christ before Caiaphas
	Also Mk 14:53-65; Lk 22:54
Mt 26:68-75	Peter denied Christ three times
	Also:Mk 14:66-72; Lk 22:55-62;Jn 18:13-27

The ossuary of "Joseph, son of Caiaphas" was recently discovered in a tomb at the Peace Forest at the Sherover Promenade near East Talpiot in southern Jerusalem. Inside were the bones of six people, including those of a 60-yr-old man, most likely Caiaphas. The ossuary is on display at the Israel Museum, Jerusalem.

Mt 26:3	Caiaphas the High Priest
Lk 3:2	Caiaphas the High Priest
Jn 11:49	Caiaphas the High Priest
Jn 18:13	Caiaphas the High Priest
Acts 4:6	Peter and John questioned

» You can't really visit the tomb, but you can get close. About half way along the promenade is a children's playground. Beside this, at the roadside, two curved and painted metal pipes protrude out of the

ground apparently over the site of the tomb.

CENACLE OR COENACULUM

Cenacle is Greek for 'supper' and coenaculum is Latin for 'dining hall' This popularly is considered to be the room of the Last Supper, that is the Upper Room, and is immediately upstairs from the Tomb of King David (Acts 2:29). According to tradition, this was the home of Mary, the mother of John Mark, and may also have been the headquarters of the early church. The Armenians claim that the site of last supper is inside today's Syrian Church of St. Mark in the Armenian Quarter (Map 1).

Mt 26:17-35	Last supper
	Also: Mk 14:12-25; Lk 22:7-38; Jn 13:1-30
Acts 1:12-26	Choosing Matthias
Acts 2:1-4	Day of Pentecost
Acts 12:12-16	Peter came after his escape from prison

TOMB OF KING DAVID

The traditional burial place of King David is immediately downstairs from the Room of the Last Supper (Acts 2:29). However, this location is highly disputed because David was 'buried in the City of David' (1 Ki 2:10). Based on Acts 13:36, some propose that King David is buried in Bethlehem.

HOUSE OF HARRARI

While this is not a Biblical site it is nevertheless of Biblical interest. The House of Harrari makes Biblical Harps, are preparing harps for the new temple, and are the first Biblical harp makers in Jerusalem in almost 2000 years.

» This store is in the new city. Walk about 75m south of Zion Sq. (junction of Ben Yehuda St. and Jaffa Rd.) along Jaffa Rd. to a narrow alley called Nahalat Shiva' St. Turn right and the store is about 70m on your left.

NORTHWARD FROM JERUSALEM (SAMARIA)

"Go forth into the north country"
(Zec 6:6)

RAMAH (ARIMATHEA)
In Ephraim
'height'

> *"A voice was heard in Ramah, lamentation and bitter weeping; Rahel weeping for her children refused to be comforted for her children, because they were not" Jer 31:15*

(Map 3). Also called Ramathaim-zophim (1 Sam 1:1). There was also a Ramah in Benjamin (Jos 18:25), Ramah in Naphtali (Jos 19:36), in Asher (Jos 19:29), in Simeon (Jos 19:8), and in Gilead (2 Ki 8:29). Some identify this site as Mizpeh and instead locate Ramah at Tel en-Nasbeh south of Ramallah. The site described here may possibly be the site of New Testament Arimathea.

1 Sam 1:19,20	Birthplace and home of Samuel
1 Sam 2:11	Elkanah lived in Ramah
1 Sam 7:17	Home of Samuel
1 Sam 8:4	Israel demanded a king
1 Sam 9:6-10	Saul first met Samuel
1 Sam 25:1	Burial place of the prophet Samuel
1 Sam 19:18	David hid from king Saul
1 Ki 15:17-21	Baasha king of Israel, fortified Ramah
1 Ki 15:22	King Asa dismantled Ramah
Jer 40:1	Jeremiah released after the exile

»About 9 km northwest of Jerusalem on route #436, and overlooking the Valley of Gibeon to the north. Follow the main road up the hill through Ramot Allon and continue for a further 2-3 km to the top of the hill. The site is easily identified by a prominent mosque. Another popular opinion is that Arimathea is located at todays village of Rantis. Rantis is located only 15 km east northeast of Ben Gurion airport just to the south of route #465, but it is quite a difficult village to get to.

GIBEON
(Maps 3&4). One of the four Hivite cities (Jos 9;7,17), a Royal

city (Jos 10:2), and a city of refuge (Jos 21:17). There is an impressive rock-cut water cistern with spiral staircase (79 steps), which is 12m diameter and about 23m deep. The area of the pool of Gibeon is called Helkath Hazzurim (2 Sam 2:15) meaning field of daggers or field of hostilities.

Jos 9:3-7	The Gibeonites deceived Joshua
Jos 10:1-6	Five Amorite kings plotted against Gibeon
Jos 10:9-13	Joshua prayed that the sun would stand still
2 Sam 2:12-17	Battle between Joab and Abner
2 Sam 3:30	Abner killed Asahel
2 Sam 20:8-10	Joab stabbed Amasa in the fifth rib
1 Ki 3:4-15	God granted Solomon wisdom
1 Chr 16:39	The Tabernacle was located here
2 Chr 1:3	Solomon came to the high place
Jer 28:1	Home of the false prophet Hananiah
Jer 41:12	Fighting at the great pool in Gibeon

» Now the Arab village of El Jib, 11 km northwest of Jerusalem, on route #437 and 2 km north of Ramah. Best access is to continue beyond the prophet Samuel's tomb on route #436 for about 2 km to the bottom of the valley. Gibeon is on your right. Turn right on route #437 to El Jib for 1.2 km. Turn right to the village and trace the road to the very top of the hill to your left - follow the map (4). At the top of the hill, the road turns quite sharp left and there is a 'natural' parking place on the outside of the corner. Walk along the rough track for about 100m to the cistern on your left. Careful, the cistern can be dangerous, especially if you use the steps, and especially if wet; all sorts of broken barbed wire fences are present to discourage you from using it. Close to the cistern (about 3m away from the northern edge) about 10m from where the spiral stairs emerge you will see a very small opening that apparently leads nowhere; it does! If you have a flash or candles, this opening leads down 91 steps into solid rock to another water system. It's safe enough if you are careful, but you do this one at your own risk.

ANATHOTH
In Benjamin, given to the Levites (Jos 21:18;1 Ki 2:26)
(Map 3)

Arise, walk through the land

2 Sam 23:27	Birthplace of Abiezer, one of David's chiefs
1 Ki 2:26	Home of Abiathar the priest
1 Chr 12:3	Birthplace of Jehu, one of David's chiefs
Jer 1:1; 29:27	Home of Jeremiah
Jer 32:6-10	Jeremiah bought a field from his cousin

» The name survives in today's Arab village of Anata about 4 km northeast of Jerusalem, just off the Jericho Rd. and close to Gibeah. The actual ruins are, apparently, about 800m to the northwest on the summit of a broad ridge of hills known as Ras el-Kharrubeh. To reach the village, go north from Jerusalem towards Ramallah. After crossing French Hill enter the large junction and turn right on route #1 towards Jericho. Travel about 1 km to the traffic lights, turn left for 0.5 km and turn right for 1 km into Anata.

GIBEAH

In Benjamin (Judg 19:14)
'the hill'
(Map 3). Arguably the same as Gibeath (Jos 18:28). The first capital of united Israel, and the residence of King Saul. Some argue that Gibeah are Geba are two different names for the same place, others argue that they are distinct places (e.g. compare 1 Sam 14:5 in King James and NIV, and 2 Sam 5:25 - but see 1 Sam 14:2, and Is 10:29).

Jos 24:33	Eleazar the high priest buried (see Awarta)
Judg 19:11-29	Homosexuality; Levite's concubine raped
Judg 20	Israelites destroyed the city
1 Sam 10:1-5	Saul met a procession of prophets
1 Sam 10:26	Royal city of Saul
1 Sam 11:4	Birthplace of Saul
1 Sam 13:15	Samuel rebuked Saul and went to Gibeah
1 Sam 13:16	Saul camped before battling Philistines
1 Sam 14:2,16	Saul camped before battling Philistines
1 Sam 15:34	The home of Saul
1 Sam 19:9,10	David played the harp; Saul tried to kill him
2 Sam 21:1-9	Gibeonites avenged; killed seven of Saul's descendants

2 Sam 23:29   Ittaithe son of Ribai from Gibeah
2 Chr 13:2   Michaiah the mother of Abijah, king of Judah,
came from Gibeah
Jer 41:11-15   Johanan went to attack Ishmael
» Most identify Gibeah as Tel El Ful, 5 km north of Jerusalem on route #60 on the east side of the road, and recognized by having the unfinished palace of King Hussein of Jordan on its summit. However, some argue that Gibeah is a different name for Geba (e.g. Jos 18:24) located at today's Arab village of Jaba (see Geba entry).

GRAVES OF THE CHILDREN OF ISRAEL

The traditional burial place of Rachel, on the northern outskirts of Bethlehem, is clearly open to dispute. In 1 Sam 10:2 it says that Rachel's tomb is in the territory of Benjamin which is located approximately between Jerusalem (Hinnom Valley) and Ramallah. Because of this, some have looked for Rachel's tomb north of Jerusalem. Just north of the village of Hizma are four huge rectangular stone structures which from ancient times have been referred to as Kubur Bani Isra'il - the Graves of the Children of Israel. Their actual origin and use is not at all clear.

Gen 48:7   Rachel buried on the way to Ephrath
1 Sam 10:2   Rachel buried in Benjamin
Jer 31:15   Rachel buried near Ramah
» Drive north from Jerusalem and follow the Ramallah by-pass. As you leave the built-up area of Jerusalem (the neighborhood of Neveh Ya'akov) you will drive around a roundabout. After 0.6 km you will come to an Israeli Army check point at a road junction. Straight on goes to Mishor Adummim, but you should turn left continuing to follow the signs to the Ramallah by-pass. After 0.6 km a road goes to the right to the village of Hizma; keep straight on for another 2.1 km. At this point the main by-pass road will be going uphill, entering and going round a left sweeping curve. Just before the curve, before the guard rail begins, the large structures can be seen just a few meters off the side of the road to the right.

Arise, walk through the land   31

GEBA

In Benjamin (Jos 18:24;21:17); a Levitical city (1 Chr 6:60).
'a hill'

(Map 3). After the division of the kingdom, Geba was considered the northern limit of Judah and so we get the phrase "from Geba to Beersheva" (2 Ki 23:8). Jonathan and his armor bearer came through, or perhaps from, Geba on their way to the battle at Michmash. Some argue that this is the actual location of Gibeah, the first capital of united Israel, and the residence of King Saul. This argument has credibility because Saul's lookouts could apparently see Michmash from Gibeah (1 Sam 14:16).

1 Sam 13:3	Jonathan attacked the Philistines
1 Sam 14:1-23	Jonathan and his armor bearer
2 Sam 5:25	David's victory over Philistines
1 Ki 15:22	King Asa fortified the city
2 Chr 16:6	King Asa fortified the city
Ezra 2:26	Part of the returning exiles
Neh 7:30	Part of the returning exiles
Neh 12:29	Dedication of the new wall in Jerusalem
Is 10:29	Invasion route of the Assyrian army
Zech 14:10	Zechariah's apocalyptic vision

» This is today's Arab village of Jaba. While driving north from Jerusalem on route #60, just before the airport, follow route #437 to the east for about 5 km until you reach the intersection to the Jerusalem bypass; Geba is immediately left of the road. Continue further along route #437 towards Michmash. As you drive this road from Geba to Michmash you should be aware that you are on the invasion route of the Assyrian army (Is 10:28, 29). The Pass of Geba was here because the gorge becomes impassable further to the east.

MICHMASH

(Map 3)

1 Sam 13:2	Saul had 2000 men to fight the Philistines
1 Sam 13:5,11,16	Philistines camped before battling Saul
Is 10:28	Invasion route of the Assyrian army

» Today's Arab village of Mukhmas east of the road from Jerusalem to Ramallah. While driving north from Jerusalem on route #60, just before the airport, follow route #437 to the east for 6 km until the sign to Mukhmas points off to the right. Drive for about 1.5 km into the village.

MIGRON

(Map 3). This one is difficult because there may have been two different towns, or places, with this name, or perhaps both references are to the same place. Migron may also have referred to the Wadi es-Swenit. If they are different they are in close proximity.

1 Sam 14:2   Saul camped before battle with Philistines
1 Sam 14:1-14   Jonathan's victory over the Philistines
Is 10:28   Invasion route of the Assyrian army

» Migron is possibly Tel Maryam about 1 km west of Michmash located on the edge of the Wadi es-Swenit. However, Tel Maryam is also tentatively identified as Beth Aven. Alternatively, Migron may be an ancient name for the wadi itself. Wadi es-Swenit ('Jonathan's gorge') is a seasonal stream about mid-way between Geba (today's Arab village of Jaba) and Michmash (today's Arab village of Mukhmas). It is immediately south of Mukhmas and is best viewed from about 0.5 km before entering the village. The right hand cliff of the gorge is called Bozez and the left is Seneh (1 Sam 14:4,5). If you get stuck, ask some of the villagers to point you in the direction of Wadi es-Swenit - better still, ask them to take you.

BETH AVEN

'house of idols' or 'house of iniquity'
(Map 3). Also spelled Beth-aven in King James. This town is near Ai (Jos 7:2), west of Michmash (1 Sam 13:5) and on the border of Benjamin (Jos 18:12). Beth Aven may be east of Bethel (Jos 7:2) or it may even be another name for Bethel; Hos 4:15, 5:8 and 10:5 used the name symbolically to refer to the idolatry of the city of Bethel i.e. the 'house of God' had become a 'house of idols' or a 'house of iniquity'

1 Sam 14:23   Israel routed the Philistines

Arise, walk through the land

» Identification is not at all certain and it may simply be another name for Bethel. However, some suggest that this is Tel Maryam which overlooks Wadi es-Swenit ('Jonathan's gorge'). As you drive along route #37 between Geba and Michmash you will descend a long sweeping hill down into the wadi. As you near the bottom of the hill, Tel Maryam is about 1 km off to your right on the left bank of the wadi. Alternatively, continue for about 1 km until you see the signpost to Mukhmas. Take this road for 0.8 km and Tel Maryam is off to the right of the road just behind a fairly new and large home.

MIZPEH

In Benjamin (1 Ki 15:22)
'watchtower'

"Ebenezer, Hitherto hath the LORD helped us"
(1 Sam 7:12)

"God save the king" (1 Sam 10:24)

(Map 3). Also Mizpah. Some identify the tomb of the prophet Samuel at Ramah (Nebi Samwil) as being Mizpeh. It is in the vicinity of Ramah and Geba (1 Ki 15:22). There is also a Mizpeh (or Mizpah) near Mount Hermon (Jos 11:3,8), in Judah (Jos 15:38), in Gilead (Judg 11:29,34), and in Moab (1 Sam 22:3).

1 Sam 7:5-17	Samuel assembled all of Israel
1 Sam 7:6	Samuel was leader of Israel at Mizpeh
1 Sam 7:16-17	On Samuel's circuit as a judge of Israel
1 Sam 10:9-25	Saul chosen as king
1 Ki 15:22	King Asa rebuilt the city
2 Ki 25:22-25	Gedaliah appointed governor
Jer 40:7-41:3	Ishmael assassinated Gedaliah

» This is Tel en-Nasbeh 10 km north of Jerusalem on route #60 on the southern edge of Ramallah. As you enter Al Bireh, the Tel is immediately to your left. To access the Tel, drive beyond (north) of it on route #60 and take the first turn up the hill to the left. Follow the road to the top of the Tel. A prominent wall on the northeast corner was built by King Asa. This may be the site of Ramah.

AL BIREH

In Benjamin (Jos 18:21,25)

(Map 3). Traditionally, this is reputed to be the point of "a day's journey" from Jerusalem. It is also identified with ancient Beeroth, and some scholars identify it as Bethel.

Jos 9:17	On the route of Joshua's conquest
2 Sam 4:2,3	Baanah and Rechab's father from Beeroth
Neh 7:5,6,29	Some of the people who returned from captivity in Babylon
Lk 2:43-52	Joseph and Mary missed Jesus

» On the southern edge of Ramallah on the road from Jerusalem.

RAMALLAH

(Map 3). An Arabic name meaning 'Height of God' and probably the 'Hill of God'. Possible site of Biblical Ramah.

1 Sam 10:5	Samuel sent Saul to Ramallah

» Ramallah is 14 km north of Jerusalem on route #60.

BETHEL

In Benjamin (Jos 18:22; Neh 11:31)

'the House of God'

(Maps 3, 5 & 6). Formerly Luz (Gen 28:19; 36:6; Jos 18:13), now Beit-El or Beitin. Also called El Bethel (Gen 35:7). Some scholars place Bethel at Al Bireh.

Gen 12:8	Abram pitched his tent and built an altar
Gen 28:10-22	Jacob's ladder
Gen 35:1-7	Jacob built an altar
Gen 35:8	Deborah, Rebekah's nurse died
Gen 35:14	Jacob set up a stone pillar
Jos 12:7-16	Joshua killed the king of Bethel
Judg 1:22-26	House of Joseph attacked Bethel
Judg 4:4-6	Deborah lived nearby
Judg 20:26,27	The ark was here for a time
1 Sam 7:16-17	On Samuel's circuit as a judge of Israel
1 Ki 12:29-32	Jeroboam set up a golden calf
1 Ki 13	Man of God prophesied against Jeroboam

1 Ki 13:1-9	Jeroboam's hand shriveled and altar split
2 Ki 2:2	Elijah and Elisha went to Bethel
2 Ki 2:23-25	Youths killed when they jeered Elisha
2 Ki 17:28	Assyrians taught how to worship God
2 Ki 23:4	Ashes of idols brought from the Kidron
2 Ki 23:15	King Josiah destroyed Jeroboam's altar
Ezra 1:1;2:28	Occupied after the return from captivity

» Bethel is to the "west of Ai" (Gen 12:8). Leave Ramallah going north on route # 60 towards Nablus. After about 1 km, route #3 turns off to the east. Follow this for 1.8 km then turn off to the right. From this junction drive through Beitin for 1.2 km until you come to an area of open ground to the left, immediately after the school. There is a rough track and the site is about 100m back from the road.

AI

(Maps 3, 5 & 6). Also called Hai (Gen 12:8; 13:3), Aiath (Is 10:28), and Aija (Neh 11:31), the name means 'The Ruin' and it is "near Beth Aven" (Jos 7:2). It is the second place attacked by the Israelites under Joshua.

Gen 12:8	Abram pitched his tent and built an altar
Jos 7:2-5	Joshua defeated because of Achan's sin
Jos 8:1-29	Joshua destroyed Ai
Ezra 1:1;2:28	Occupied after the return from captivity

» Today's Et-Tell, at the village of Deir Dibwan, about 2 km "east of Bethel" (Gen 12:8; Jos 7:2), although previously proposed to have been either Khirbet Haiyan at the southern edge of Deir Dibwan, or Khirbet Khudriya 2 km east of Deir Dibwan. From the ruins of Bethel continue for 1.2 km to a junction. Turn left under the new bridge and continue 2.3 km to the village of Deir Dibwan. From the turning circle in the center of the village, follow map 5.

BAAL HAZOR

Near the border of Ephraim
(Maps 3 & 6)
2 Sam 13:23-29 Absalom's men killed Amnon

»A prominent mountain (Tell Asur), 1016m high, about 3 km northeast of the Jewish settlement of Ofra on route #3, 5 km beyond Beitin. It is the highest point in the mountains of Ephraim. Best view is from the top of the hill about 0.9 km beyond Ofra.

OPHRAH

In Benjamin (Jos 18:23)
(Map 6). This may also be Ephron (2 Chr 13:19) translated as Ephraim in some places (2 Sam 13:23).
1 Sam 13:17   A Philistine raiding party came here
» Today's Arab village of Et-Taybeh 9 km from Bethel on route #3 towards Jericho. El-Taybeh is 6.5 km beyond the Jewish settlement of Ofra on route #3.

BAAL SHALISHA

(Map 6). Also called Shalisha (1 Sam 9:4)
1 Sam 9:4   Saul searched for lost donkeys
2 Ki 4:42-44   Baal Shalisha man brought bread to Elisha
» About 4 km north of the Jewish settlement of Ofra, turn left (northeast) towards Kafr Malik. Continue through Kafr Malik along an especially scenic road to the junction with route #458. Turn left (north) and after 200m at the valley bottom, turn left again unto a rough road. The ruins of Khirbet el-Marjama are on top of the low hill to your right; this may be the location of Baal Shalisha but cannot be identified with certainty.

ARIMATHEA

'a height'
Arimathaea in King James. This is possibly today's Arab village of Rantis, and some Christian tradition also places it at the town of Ramla, near Ben Gurion airport. It was the hometown of Joseph, a member of the Jewish Sanhedrin in Jerusalem, in whose tomb Jesus was laid.
Mt 27:57   Joseph, a rich man from Arimathea
See Mk15:43; Lk 23:50-1; Jn 19:38, 39
» To get to Rantis, drive about 12 km north of Ramallah on route #60 until you see a sign to the left to Halamish. Follow this road (route

#465) for 28 km (see Timnath Serah entry - Kh. Timneh). The main road takes a sharp right turn at a gas station. At this corner take the minor road to the left and travel the short distance in to the village which has two mosques with brightly colored domes. Alternatively, approach from the south and west; from Ben Gurion airport follow routes #40, 461 and 465 for about 17 km. Ramla is close to Ben Gurion airport and has a Church of St. Nichodemus and Joseph Arimathea (also see Ramah entry).

SHILOH
In Ephraim
This is where Israel set up the tabernacle soon after arriving in Canaan, although the ark was at Bethel for a time (Judg 20:26,27). Shiloh became the center of Israel's worship, and the tent was replaced by a more permanent building.

Jos 18:1-10	Tribes received their inheritance
Jos 18:8,9	The land and its cities surveyed
Judg 21:19	Annual festival at Shiloh
1 Sam 1:1-9	Elkanah, Hannah, Eli at the Lord's temple
1 Sam 1:3	Home of Hophni and Phinehas
1 Sam 3	Childhood of Samuel
1 Sam 4:4-11	Ark of the Covenant captured
1 Ki 14:2	Jeroboam's wife went to Ahijah

» Now called Seilun, 20 km north of Ramallah on route #60, and 16 km "north of Bethel and east of the road that goes from Bethel to Shechem, and to the south of Lebonah" (Judg 21:19). Follow the signs to the settlement of Shiloh and then follow the signs to the Tel.

LEBONAH
In Ephraim (Judg 21:19)
'incense'

Judg 21:19	Wives for some Benjamites

» Perhaps todays village of Lubban situated just to the west of the main highway from Jerusalem to Nablus (Shechem) about 5 km north of Shiloh.

TIMNATH SERAH

In Ephraim (Judg 24:30)

'portion of the sun'

(Map 7). A city in the mountains of Ephraim north of the mountains of Gaash (Jos 24:30). Also called Timnath Hares (Judg 2:9) but this may simply be a misspelling of 'Serah' spelled backwards. Timnath Serah is where Joshua was buried and there are at least three traditions concerning this location; one of these is primarily a Shi'ite Moslem tradition and locates Joshua's tomb about 10 km north of Hazor. The other two locations are described below the scripture texts.

Jos 19:49, 50   Joshua's inheritance, and home

Jos 24:29, 30   Joshua died at age of 110, and was buried

Kifl Harit

Within this village are three separate tombs which, according to Jewish, Samaritan and Moslem tradition, are purported to be those of Nun (Joshua's father), Joshua and Caleb. Nun obviously died before entering the Promised Land (Num 14:26-33). His body must have been brought along when the people of Israel entered the land although there is no Biblical record of this.

» Turn west off route #60 on to route #505. Drive about 9 km to the village of Kifl Harit. The village is well signposted and is about 1 km to the north of the main highway. The tombs are not so well signposted although they are all labeled when you find them! Upon entering the village follow map 7. Caleb's tomb comes first and is easily recognized by the double green domes of the small mosque. Continue uphill to Joshua's tomb. Leave your car here and don't even think of trying to drive to Nun's tomb - it's only about 250m. Follow the road beyond Joshua's tomb; it soon becomes a bumpy track, then ends apparently nowhere, and a small pathway continues for about another 50m - and there it is - easy!

Khirbet Tibneh

» Drive about 12 km north of Ramallah on route #60 until you see a sign to the left to Halamish. Follow this road (route #465) for 12-14

km until you come to a strange 4-way junction just beyond the first turn-off to Halamish. At this junction the main road makes a fairly sharp hairpin bend. About 2 km further you will notice Kh. Tibneh off to the left of the road. It is identifiable by four large and very obvious rock-hewn tombs about 100m of the road and along an unmarked gravel road to the village of Deir Nidham. If you should miss this you will know you have gone too far when you see a signpost to Deir Abu Mashal - retrace your path from this junction for 2.5 km. The locals call these tombs Bet el-Hadad. I can't be definite on this but we were told that Joshua's tomb was the one slightly higher up the slope than the first two; this is square-cut and inside there are 15 different naves, one being much larger than the others - bring a flashlight!

AWARTA

An Arab village about 6 km southeast of Shechem (Nablus) and on the road to Yanun. The village has three tombs purportedly connected to the priestly family of Moses' brother, Aaron; these are (i) Eleazar, (ii) Ithamar, Aaron's son, and brother of Eleazar , and (iii) Phinehas, Abishua and the 70 elders who helped Moses bear the burden of caring for the people (Num 11:16-17). The only problem with this identification is that according to Jos 24:33, Eleazar was buried at Gibeah!

Eleazar

Aaron's first two sons, Nadab and Abihu, were killed for offering unholy fire to the Lord (Lev 10:1-7). Eleazar and his brother Ithamar were consecrated as priests in place of the two elder brothers. There are at least six other Eleazar's in the Bible: 1. Son of Abinadab (1 Sam 7:1). 2. Son of Dodai (1 Chr 11:12). 3. Of the house of Merari (1 Chr 23:21). 4. A priest/musician (Neh 12:42). 5. Son of Phinehas (Ezra 8:33). 6. The son of Eliud and ancestor of Jesus (Mt 1:15).

Ex 6:23	The third son of Aaron and Elisheba
	(Also: Num 3:2; 26:60; 1 Chr 6:4; 4:1)
Ex 6:25	The father of Phinehas (Num 25:7)

Ex 28:1	Consecrated as a priest
Num 3:4	Served as a priest
Num 3:32	The chief leader of the Levites
Num 4:16	In charge of the entire tabernacle
Num 20:25	Ascended Mount Hor with Aaron
Num 20:25-28	Invested with Aaron's high priestly garments
Num 26:63	Counted Israelites on the plains of Moab
Num 27:18-22	Joshua to succeed Moses
Num 34:17	Assigned the land as an inheritance
Jos 19:51	Divided the land at Shiloh

Ithamar

Ex 6:23	The fourth son of Aaron and Elisheba (Also: Num 3:2; 26:60; 1 Chr 6:3; 24:1)
Ex 28:1	Consecrated as a priest
Ex 38:21	He numbered the articles for the tabernacle
Num 3:4	Served as a priest (1 Chr 24:2)
Num 4:28, 33	Supervised Gershonites and Merarites at the Tent of meeting

Phinehas

The third high priest of Israel. There are at least two other Phinehas's in the Old Testament: 1. The younger of the two sons of Eli the priest (1 Sam. 1:3). 2. The father of Eleazar (Ezra 8:33).

Ex 6:25	A son of Eleazar and grandson of Aaron
Num 25	He killed Zimri and Cozri
Num 25:11-13	Promised a permanent priesthood
Jos 22:13-32	Went to Reuben, Gad and the half-tribe of Manasseh.
1 Chr 6:4	Phinehas the father of Abishua
1 Chr 9:20	In charge of the gatekeepers

Abishua

The fourth high priest of Israel (1 Chr. 6:4-5).

1 Chr 6:4	Was the son of Phinehas
1 Chr 6:5	Was the father of Bukki

» Drive about 4 km south of Nablus on route #60. Turn east on route #507 towards Awarta. Just as you enter the village and before you start climbing the long winding hill, a rough track turns off to the right. Take this turn and follow the track for 300m, turn right again and you will come to the tomb of Eleazar in a walled enclosure at the end of the track. Next retrace your tracks to the road and go up hill to the center of the village to the tomb of Ithamar. Just a little further on the left, on the east of the village (ask the locals for directions) is a two-domed structure. Phinehas and Abishua are apparently buried in the main tomb and the 70 elders in the cave behind the tomb.

JANOAH
In Ephraim (Jos 16:6,7)
'rest'
Todays Arab village of Yanun to the southeast of Shechem.
» Drive about 4 km south of Hebron on route #60. Turn east on route #507 towards Awarta and Yanun.

SHECHEM
'shoulder'
> *"Choose you this day whom ye will serve...As for me and my house, we will serve the LORD" (Jos 24:15)*

(Map 8). Also called Sichem (Gen 12:6). In Roman times it was called Neapolis. It is situated between Mount Ebal to the north and Mount Gerizim to the south. This was the first place Abram visited in Palestine, and was the first capital of the northern kingdom of Israel (1 Ki 12:25). Some scholars identify Sychar as Shechem. Sychar is "near to the parcel of land that Jacob gave to his son Joseph" (Jn 4:5) which was within site of the city of Shechem (Gen 33:18,19). Shechem was a city of refuge (Jos 20:7;21:21).

Gen 12:6-7	Abram passed through on his way from Ur
Gen 33:18-20	Jacob built an altar and dug a well
Gen 34	Dinah defiled, and revenge by her brothers
Gen 34:22-25	All the men of Shechem were circumcised
Gen 37:12-16	Joseph went to look for his brothers

Jos 24:1-28	Joshua renewed the Covenant
Jos 24:32	Joseph's bones returned from Egypt*
Judg 8:29-31	Birthplace of Gideon's son, Abimelech
Judg 9:1-5	Abimelech revolts against his brothers
Judg 9:6	Abimelech made king
1 Ki 12:1	Rehoboam crowned king
1 Ki 12:2-20	Rebellion against Rehoboam; kingdom divided
1 Chr 10:1	Rehoboam made king
1 Chr 10	Israel rebelled against Rehoboam
Acts 7:15-16	Joseph buried**

* *Josephus explains that Joseph's bones were later transferred from Shechem to the Tombs of the Patriarchs at the Cave of Machpelah in Hebron.*

** *It is Jewish tradition that the brothers and sons of Joseph were also returned from Egypt to Shechem.*

» This is today's Tel Balatah at the eastern end of the modern Arab city of Nablus. The most prominent attraction today are the major walls dated to about 1600BC. The Orthodox church which houses Jacob's Well is about 400m to the southeast - best to ask for directions.

SYCHAR

(Map 8). A city of Samaria associated with Jesus' visit to Jacob's well. Jacob's well is 35m deep and is at the eastern end of Nablus (see Shechem entry). Some scholars identify Sychar with Shechem.

Jn 4:1-26	Jesus and the woman at Jacob's well

» The name is carried on today as the village (suburb) of Askar as one is leaving Nablus on route #55 to Adam Bridge and Jericho. In the village is a magnificent Samaritan tomb with nine sarcophagi. Most locals want to send you to Joseph's tomb and they don't seem to have a name for this particular tomb. Follow map 8 and it's reasonably easy to find.

MOUNT GEREZIM AND MOUNT EBAL

Two mountains facing each other at either side of Shechem (modern Nablus). Mt. Gerezim (869m) to the south is the 'Mountain of God's Blessing' and Mt. Ebal (939m) to the north is the 'Mountain of God's curses', that is, the blessings for keeping the law and the curses for not keeping it. Mt. Gerezim became the Samaritan's sacred mountain and they believe it to be Biblical Mt. Moriah (but see 2 Chr 3:1). The Samaritans consider Mt. Ebal an accursed mountain. A ledge halfway up Mt. Gerezim is referred to as Jotham's pulpit.

Deut 11:26-32   People given choice to obey or disobey
Deut 27:11-14   Twelve tribes assembled on the mountains
Jos 8:33   Israel assembled on the two mountains
Judg 9:7-20   Jotham spoke to the people of Shechem against Abimelech
Jn 4:19-20   Jesus and the Samaritan woman

» Simply drive to the top of Mt. Gerezim but be sure you have a good first gear and good brakes. Near the top you will arrive in a well-manicured little settlement. Straight ahead you will see extensive, mostly Byzantine, ruins. To the north of these ruins (actually quite lower on the hill) is the fairly prominent Tel Er Ras where the Samaritans believe Abraham sacrificed Isaac. It's an easy walk across the boulder-strewn hillside. In the village you will see a small grocery store beside what looks to be a small park. This small park is the location where the Samaritans sacrifice their Passover animals. Ask the manager in the store for an explanatory booklet.

JOSHUA'S ALTAR ON MT. EBAL

Deut 27:4-8   The altar on Mt. Ebal
Jos 8:30   Joshua built an altar on Mt. Ebal.

»If you are able, you absolutely must make the effort to get to this altar. It is a walk of approximately 3.5 - 4 km, or 40mins, each way. Unfortunately it is easier to get there than to get back when you have a few uphill climbs. To get to the site I will give directions from the Jewish settlement of Shave Shomeron. However, if you can find another way to the top of Mt. Ebal, that's OK. Shave Shomeron is

about 1 km north of the junction of routes 60 and 57 as you travel from Nablus to Samaria. Opposite the entrance to Shave Shomeron is a newly constructed road. Drive along this road for 7 km to a T-junction; turn right for 1 km until you come to a hairpin bend in the road. At this bend take the road to the left and head straight up the long hill. After 3.2 km, and when you are within sight of the entrance to the military installation, you will find a dirt 'road' taking off to the right. Park here. Leave a note on your dash board explaining where you are! Now start walking at a moderate pace for about 40 minutes - there is only one junction in the road and when you reach it, it is obvious that you should turn right, because left brings you back into the military area. At one point in your walk the road takes a sharp right bend and drops straight downhill for about 200m at the bottom of which is a right angle bend to the left. Turn the corner and look straight ahead - the altar is on top of the mound about 400-500m straight in front of you. The altar is made of uncut stones and is about 1-2m high and about 5m on a side. Follow the road as far as you are able and then clamber the final few meters to the altar.

OAK OF MOREH
'diviner'

On the summit of Mount Kabir (Jebel Kheiber), just below a Muslim tomb, is a huge spreading oak tree. This is believed by some to be Biblical Elon Moreh - the great tree of Moreh (NIV), or plain of Moreh (KJ). If this is true then this is the place where God promised the land to Abram on his first journey through Canaan. This may have been the same tree under which Jacob hid the false gods (Gen 35:4), and where Joshua erected a large memorial stone when Israel renewed its covenant with God. The name Moreh also applies to a mountain on the northern edge of the Jezreel valley.

Gen 12:6, 7   God promised the land to Abram
Deut 11:26-32   Trees are near Mt. Ebal and Mt. Gerezim
Jos 24:26   Joshua erected a commemorative stone

» This location cannot be determined accurately. However, the name is continued today by the village of Elon Moreh about 5 km east of

Shechem. Elon is the Hebrew word for 'oak'. Just beyond the village is Mt. Kabir (Jebel Kheibir) is a large, a very old (perhaps 500 years) oak tree. Drive along the Nablus by-pass from route #60 and #56. Almost immediately east of Nablus you will see signposts to Elon Moreh to the east. From this junction drive to the Jewish settlement of Elon Moreh and ask for directions to get you through the settlement and on to the top of Har Kabir.

TIRZAH

'delightfulness'
Capital of the northern kingdom of Israel until Omri moved the capital to Samaria (1 Ki 16:24). Most of Israel's kings from Jeroboam I to Omri, reigned and were buried at Tirzah (mostly recorded in 1 Kings 14-16).

Jos 12:24	Conquered by Joshua
1 Ki 14:1-18	Jeroboam's son, Abijah, died
1 Ki 15:21	Baasha, king of Israel, went to live in Tirzah
1 Ki 15:33	Baasha was king of Israel for 24 years.
1 Ki 16:9	King Elah drunk in the home or Arza
1 Ki 16:9-13	Zimri killed Baasha's family
1 Ki 16:23	Omri reigned in Tirzah six years
Song 6:4	Thou art beautiful, O my love, as Tirzah

»The ruins of Tel el-Fara are situated about 12 km northeast of Nablus. From Nablus, follow route #12 north for 5 km to a water park and garden. About 0.8 km beyond the park, turn north (left) on route #588 towards Tubas. After 4.8 km you will go down a fairly steep hill, sharp right over a small stream and an immediate track off to the left. Take this track straight on to the tel.

THEBEZ

Judg 9:50-55   Abimelech killed
» Thought by many scholars to be today's modern village of Tubas, about 5 km north of Tirzah at the junction with route #5799.

BEZEK

A town allotted to the tribe of Judah (Judg 1:4-5)
'lightning'

Judg 1:4   Residence of Adoni-Bezek
1 Sam 11:8   Saul mustered 330,000 men

» This is usually identified as Khirbet Ibzik, north of Tubas on route #588. About 1 km south of Akaba a dirt road turns east and runs for 5-6 km to the top of a hill where the ruins are, apparently, on each side of the road. I confess, we didn't pursue this one.

SAMARIA

*"Then Elisha said....tomorrow about this time
shall a measure of fine flour be sold for a
sheckel, and two measures of barley for a
sheckel, in the gate of Samaria" (2 Ki 7:1)*

After the capital of the northern kingdom of Israel had moved from Shechem, to Penuel, and to Tirzah, it finally moved to Samaria. Samaria was built about 800 BC by Omri (1 Ki 16:24). Most of Israel's kings reigned, and were buried, in Samaria (mostly recorded in 2 Kings). There are over 120 scriptures references to either the city of Samaria or the region of Samaria. The adjacent village of Sebastia has a mosque/church which has the reputed tombs of Elisha and Obadiah (see 1 Ki 18:1-16). In addition it claims to have the headless body of John the Baptist. His head is supposedly buried in the Omayyad mosque in the old city of Damascus. Near the summit of the mound of Samaria is a small church dedicated to John the Baptist. Somehow this is linked to the discovery of John's missing head!

1 Ki 16:24   City built by Omri, king of Israel
1 Ki 16:29   Ahab, son of Omri, king of Israel
1 Ki 16:31   Ahab married Jezebel
1 Ki 16:32-33   Ahab built a temple to Baal
1 Ki 18:1-6   Famine during the time of Obadiah
1 Ki 20:1-34   Ahab defeated Ben-Hadad king of Syria
1 Ki 22:10   Prophets before the kings of Israel and Judah

1 Ki 22:33,37,38	Ahab killed; blood washed from his chariot
2 Ki 1:2	Ahaziah injured when he fell through lattice
2 Ki 6:18-23	Elisha brought Syrian army to Samaria
2 Ki 6:24-29	Famine because of the siege by Ben-Hadad of Syria
2 Ki 10	Jehu killed Ahab's family and priests of Baal
2 Ki 13:20-21	Dead man came to life when thrown into Elisha's tomb
2 Ki 17:5-6	City fell to Shalmaneser of Assyria
2 Ki 18:9,10	People deported to Assyria
Hos 7:1	A wicked city
Mic 1:5,6	Judgment against the city
Acts 8:5	Philip preached in Samaria
Acts 8:9-13	Philip baptized Simon the sorcerer
Acts 8:14	Peter and John came to the city

» About 12 km west of Nablus on routes #57 and 60 to Jenin. If you drive to the site through the village of Sebastia, make sure you return to the main road by the second road which leaves by the southern side of the main car park. This road drives right along the impressive colonnaded street.

DOTHAN
In Manasseh
'wells'

Gen 37:17-28	Joseph sold into slavery
2 Ki 6:13-23	Elisha's vision; heavenly horses and chariots
2 Ki 6:18	Syrian forces blinded by God

» Now known as Tel Dotha and situated 19 km north of the city of Samaria on route #60. An alternative location is sometimes proposed on Kibbutz Ammi'ad about 1 km north of Ammi'ad junction on route #90, about 6 km north of the Sea of Galilee.

JENIN

Overlooking the Jezreel Valley just north of Samaria. Jenin is identified with Beth Haggan and possibly the site of ancient En Gannim (Jos 19:21) meaning "the spring of gardens." It is considered to be on the border of Galilee and Samaria.

2 Ki 9:27-28   Jehu pursued Ahaziah king of Judah

Lk 17:11-19   Jesus healed the ten lepers (traditional site)

SOUTHWARD FROM JERUSALEM

*"They went out to the south of Judah,
even to Beersheba"*
2 Sam 24:7

BETHANY

'house of unripe figs'
The home of Mary, Martha and Lazarus. Some identify this as Ananiah (Neh 11:32). This is also the place where Jesus raised Lazarus.

Mt 21:17	Jesus spent some nights here
	Also: Mk 11:11
Mt 26:6-13	The anointing at Bethany
	Also: Mk 14:3-9; Jn 12:1-8
Mk 11:12-14	Jesus cursed the fig tree
	Also: Mt 21:18-21
Mk 14:3	Home of Simon the leper
Lk 10:38-42	Mary and Martha, the better part
Lk 24:50,51	Jesus ascended to heaven from near here
Jn 11:1-44	Death and resurrection of Lazarus

» This is now called el-Azariyeh, and located 3 km (Jn 11:18) east of Jerusalem, on route #1, on the eastern slope of the Mount of Olives. About 30m uphill from the church is the tomb of Lazarus. If you want to take a beautiful hike, walk uphill from the tomb for about 50m to where the road turns sharp right. Follow this quite steep road up the Mt. Of Olives for about 1 km. Here the main road turns left, but you should keep walking straight along the rough track. You will walk along between two quite high walls for about 1 km until you emerge at the Church at Bethphage. Turn past the front of the church and keep walking - all the time uphill - until you reach the top of the Mt. Of Olives. From here you can descend the western slope of the Mt. Olives past the Church of Dominus Flevit, the Church of Mary Magdalene, and the Garden of Gethsemane.

BETHPHAGE

'house of unripe figs'

Mt 21:1-3	The triumphal entry
	Also: Mk 11:1-3; Lk 19:29-31

» A village near Bethany and only a few minutes walk to the east of the Russian Church of the Ascension on top of the Mount of Olives. Probably on the site of today's village of et-Tur.

EIN YAEL (PHILIP'S SPRING)
'Spring of the Ibex'
Acts 8:26-39 tells how Philip baptized the Ethiopian eunuch. The specific location of the baptism is not given but it was on a road leading from Jerusalem to Gaza. A number of traditional sites have been proposed and they are located along the two possible roads that the eunuch could have taken - one was from Jerusalem south through Hebron to Beersheva and Gaza, the other southwestward from Jerusalem. Along the first route, a popular location is Ein-Dirwa (see Philip's Spring entry). Along the second route, Ein Yael is a strong candidate. Other locations along this route are Ein Hanniya about 2 km west of Ein Yael, and in the Wadi el-Hasi between Beit Guvrin and Gaza.

» Ein Yael is in the valley of Rephaim (Baca valley). Drive to the west of Jerusalem to the shopping mall at Malha or the Teddy stadium. Drive south past the mall (on the right) and stadium (on the left). After about 200m turn right and follow the signs to "Ein Yael Living Museum"; it's only about 1 km.

BACA VALLEY
'valley of weeping' or 'valley of Balsam trees'
Not well established but this is possibly the beautiful valley of Rephaim along which runs the railway between Jerusalem and Beth Shemesh.

2 Sam 5:18,22   Philistines encamped against David
                      Also: 2 Sam 23:13; 1 Chr 11:15
Ps 84:5-7   On pilgrimage route to Mt. Zion

» You can drive a small part of the Rephaim valley in the area close by Ein Yael, but to see it properly you should take the train from Jerusalem!

BET HAKKEREM
'house of the vineyard'
Previously identified to be at Ein Kerem but now refuted. The name is carried on in a western suburb of Jerusalem but this

---

has no connection with the site. Early excavations at the real mound showed that from the eight or ninth century B.C. there was a royal stronghold surrounded by gardens and farmhouses.

Neh 3:14   Malchiah helped repair Jerusalem
Jer 6:1   A fire-signal hill south of Jerusalem

» The mound of Ramat Rahel is situated on a prominent hill about midway between Jerusalem and Bethlehem, to the east side of the road. The site is now occupied by kibbutz Ramat Rahel. Enter the kibbutz, park by the offices, ask permission, and walk a short distance to the ruins at the back of the kibbutz.

BETHLEHEM

In Judah (Ruth 1:1)
'house of bread'
> *"Man looks on the outward appearance, but the*
> *LORD looks at the heart" (1 Sam 16:7)*

Also called Ephrath (Gen 35:19, 48:7), Ephratah (Mic 5:2) and the city of David. There is another Bethlehem in Zebulun (Jos 19:15) about 10 km west of Nazareth.

Judg 10:8-10   Judge Izban born and buried
Ruth 1:1-2   The home of Elimelech, Naomi's husband
Ruth 1:19-22   Naomi and Ruth returned from Moab
1 Sam 17:12   Family line of David
1 Sam 16:1-13   David was anointed king by Samuel
1 Sam 16:18-22   David was from Bethlehem
2 Sam 2:32   Asahel, killed by Abner, was buried here
2 Chr 11:5,6   Rehoboam fortified Bethlehem
Mic 5:2   Prophesy of the Messiah's birth
Mt 2:1-8   Birth of Jesus; Church of the Nativity
LK 2:1-7   Birth of Jesus

» Bethlehem is about 8 km southwest of Jerusalem, on route #60, in the Judean Hills. The Church of the Nativity and Manager Square are easy to find. In a cave beneath the church Jerome translated the Hebrew Bible into Latin (the so-called Vulgate).

DAVID'S WELLS

2 Sam 23:13-17 David wanted water from the well

» *David's wells are a 10min walk from Manger Square; with your back to the Church of the Nativity you will see a mosque directly across Manger Square. Take the street to the right of the mosque for 100m, turn right and follow the winding road for about 600m, right again for 100m and you will see the large gates in front of you. The wells are in the parking lot of the old cinema. If you have better things to do, don't waste your time on this one. There are three wells, one of them half buried in the growth. They each have locked covers with tiny slits for you to look down - singularly uninspiring.*

RACHEL'S TOMB

The area of Rachel's tomb is called Zelzah (1 Sam 10:2).

Gen 35:16-18   Benjamin born to Rachel
Gen 35:19   Death of Rachel
Gen 35:19   The tomb of Rachel

» *The traditional location of Rachel's tomb is on the northern end of Bethlehem on the main road to Jerusalem, about 600 hundred meters before the army checkpoint. However, the location of Rachel's tomb is disputed (see Graves of the Children of Israel) and it is probably north of Jerusalem because 1 Sam 10:2 says that Rachel's tomb was in Benjamin.*

THE SHEPHERDS' FIELDS

Ruth 2   Ruth and Boaz
Lk 2:8-15   The shepherds' fields

»*About 1 km to the east of Bethlehem is the village of Beit Sahur. Just beyond are two contenders for the Shepherds' fields. The Greek Orthodox church (with the adjacent field of Ruth and Boaz) comes first, and a little further on the Roman Catholic site. The Greek's have built a new church adjacent to the original church; the wall paintings inside the new church are well worth a visit.*

SOLOMON'S POOLS

The larger, empty pool, was built by Suleiman the magnificent, and the two smaller pools by Herod. Some erroneously link the construction of these pools to King Solomon. From these pools water flowed north through a channel directly to the Temple Mount in Jerusalem. There was not a single tributary off this channel and the water was for the exclusive use of the priests.

Eccl 2:6   Solomon built pools of water

» *About 8 km south of Beit Jala, take the road to the east towards Artas. Drive for about 300m and the pools are located on the right. Walk uphill from the middle pool for about 50m and you will see some of the ancient water conduits which brought water to the pools.*

CAVE OF ADULLAM

'refuge'

The cave that frequently served as secret headquarters for David especially when he was 'running' from Saul.

1 Sam 22:1   David and his men at the cave
1 Chr 11:15   David as a fugitive from king Saul
Ps 57 & 142   Written in the cave

» *Tradition locates the cave in the Judean wilderness 3 km south of Herodian and to the east of route #356 in Wadi Khareitun. Quite difficult to find, but best to go into the Jewish settlement of Tekoa and ask for directions. From here it is about a 3 km walk. 1 Chr 11:15 refers to the rock at the cave of Adullam; a large rock at the entrance to this cave adds some strength to the claim.*

BERACHAH

A valley in the south of the territory of Judah

'blessing'

Also spelled Beracah or Bracha. King Jehoshaphat named this place to bless the Lord after the defeat of his enemies.

2 Chr 20:26   Jehoshaphat and people blessed the Lord

» *The Berachah Valley, crosses route #60 about 10 km north of Hebron and about 2 km south of the junction with route #367.*

TEKOA

In Judah (1 Chr. 2:24; 4:5)
'trumpet blast'
Identified with Khirbet Tequa.

2 Chr 11:5,6   Rehoboam fortified Tekoa
Neh 3:5   People helped rebuild walls of Jerusalem
Amos 1:1   Home of Amos the prophet

» A small town in the Judean Hills about 9 km south of Bethlehem on route #356 and about 4 km south of the Cave of Adullam.

KEILAH

In Judah (Jos 15:44)
(Map 9)

1 Sam 23:1   Philistines attacked after harvest time
1 Sam 23:1-5   David and his men attacked the Philistines
1 Sam 23:7-13   Saul pursued David to the city
Neh 3:17,18   Rulers of Keilah aided in restoring the wall
of Jerusalem

» Today identified as Khirbet Kila. This is 10 km west on route #355 from Hebron and then 3 km north on route #354. Leave Beit Aula going west. After about 2 km the main road turns sharp right with a minor road going straight on. Take the minor road and follow map 9.

VALLEY OF ESHCOL

Part of the route taken by the spies sent out by Moses from Kadesh Barnea. Vineyards in this area are still famous for the quality of their grapes. The symbol of two men carrying a large cluster of grapes on a pole between their shoulders is used by the Israeli Ministry of Tourism.

Num 13:22-23   Spies gathered a cluster of grapes
Num 32:9   Spies viewed the land
Deut 1:24   Spies explored the valley

» About 6 km north of Hebron on route #60 the road passes through a small valley. As you enter this valley you will pass the village of Beit Zur to the west and the traditional site of Philip's spring on the

*right hand side of the road (see next two entries). You are entering
the Valley of Eshcol.*

PHILIP'S SPRING

*In Arabic the spring is named Ein-Dirwa. Another opinion is
that Philip's spring is at Ein Yael, 8 km west of the Old City of
Jerusalem in the Rephaim valley.*

Acts 8:26-39   Philip baptized the Ethiopian eunuch

*» Driving south from Bethlehem to Hebron you will cross the
Berachah Valley then pass by the village of Beit Ummar at the
junction of routes # 60 and 3527. Drive south of this junction for 4.2
km and the spring is immediately beside the left side of the road in
front of a mosque.*

BEIT ZUR

In Judah (Jos 15:58)

1 Chr 2:42-45   Inhabited by the sons of Caleb
2 Chr 11:7   Fortified by Rehoboam
Neh 3:16   During the restoration this was
                    an administrative center

*» This is Khirbet et-Tubeiqah and the Biblical name is retained in
todays Arab village about 6 km north of Hebron on route #60 just to
the west of the road. It is immediately across the road and high on
the hill opposite Philip's spring.*

HEBRON

In Judah (Jos 15:54;20:7) and given to the Levites (Jos 21:11)
'alliance'

*A city of refuge (Jos 21:13), Hebron (modern Arab city of
el-Khalil) is about 30 km south of Jerusalem on the road to
Beersheva. It is in the Judean Hills and is the highest town in
Israel at about 930m above sea level. Hebron is also referred
to as Mamre (Gen 23:19) and as Kiriath Arba (Gen 23:2; Jos
14:15).*

Gen 37:5-11   Joseph's dreams
Num 13:22   Spies sent by Moses came through
Jos 10:3-27   Joshua killed Hoham king of Hebron

Jos 14:13,14	Hebron became the inheritance of Caleb
2 Sam 2:1-4	David anointed king over Judah
2 Sam 2:11	David reigned for 7.5 years
	(7 yrs, 1 Chr 29:27)
2 Sam 3:2-5	David's six sons born including Amnon,
	Absalom and Adonijah
2 Sam 5:1-5	David anointed king over Israel
2 Sam 15:7-11	The revolt of Absalom

There are three attractions near the city center. The main attraction is the Tomb of the Patriarchs, also called the Cave of Machpelah (Haram el-Khalil in Arabic). This is a Jewish synagogue (monuments to Abraham, Sarah, Isaac and Leah, and Joseph*) and Moslem mosque (Isaac and Rebekah). Immediately outside the Jewish entrance is the Tomb of Abner. About 200m to the west on the main street is the Pool of the Sultan (in Arabic, Birket es-Sultan) identified by some as the place where David hanged the assassins of Ishbosheth, the son of Saul.

* *It is Moslem tradition that Joseph was buried in Hebron. There is also a memorial tomb to Joseph at Shechem. Josephus explains that Joseph's bones were transferred from Shechem to the Tombs of the Patriarchs at the Cave of Machpelah in Hebron.*

Tomb of the Patriarchs

Gen 23:1-2	Death of Sarah
Gen 23:17-20	Abraham bought the Cave of Machpelah
Gen 23:19	Sarah buried
Gen 25:8-10	Abraham buried
Gen 35:27-29	Isaac buried
Gen 49:31	Rebekah and Leah buried
Gen 50:12-14	Jacob buried

Tomb of Abner

2 Sam 3:27   Abner was killed by Joab and was buried
2 Sam 4:12   Ishbosheth's head buried

Pool of the Sultan

2 Sam 4:8   Ishbosheth's head brought to David
2 Sam 4:12   The assassins of Ishbosheth hanged

MAMRE

Gen 13:18   Abram moved to live in Hebron
Gen 14:13,24   Named after Mamre, an Amorite
Gen 15:5-21   Covenant of the pieces*
Gen 17:5   Abram's name changed to Abraham
Gen 18:1-15   Abraham met three visitors; promised a son
Gen 35:27   Jacob and Isaac sojourned here

Another tradition claims that this important Covenant between Abram and God took place in the Hermon mountain range.

» The ruins of the Plain (or oaks) of Mamre are located about 3 km to the north of Hebron, on the road leading to Kiryat Arba. The site has an old well, the ruins of a church and a Roman enclosure wall. As you enter the compound, straight ahead you will see a fairly large hole, or gap in the pavement (actually this paved area is the atrium) and this gap is assumed to be the original location of Abraham's terebinth. From the Roman period until the Middle Ages a tree grew in the atrium and was identified with Abraham's oak tree. Another source has the oak of Abraham (Hebrew: Eshel-Avraham) located at the Russian Church about 2 km west of Hebron on the road to Taffuh; the tree is braced and strapped to support it but is apparently only about 600 years old - personally I think it is dead.

ADORAIM

Identified as todays village of Dura to the southwest of Hebron.
2 Chr 11:9   City fortified by Rehoboam

» Drive south from Hebron on route #60 towards Beersheva. About 4 km south you will come to a crossroads with a gas station on the northeast corner. Turn east for Yatta (next entry), but turn west for 4 km to Dura.

JUTTAH

In Judah (Jos 15:55)
This is the modern city of Yatta about 8 km south of Hebron. In Lk 1:39 some commentators read 'City of Juttah" rather than "City of Judah'.
Jos 21:16   A Levitical city
» See directions to the previous (Dura) and following (Carmel) entries.

CARMEL

In Judah (Jos 15:55)
'fruit garden, orchard'
(Map 10)
1 Sam 15:12   Saul built a monument to himself
1 Sam 25:2,3   Nabal, wife of Abigail, had property
1 Sam 25:4-13   Nabal refused hospitality to David's servants
1 Sam 25:14-35 Abigail made peace with David
1 Sam 25:36-38 The Lord struck Nabal dead
1 Sam 25:39-42 David took Abigail to be his wife
2 Sam 23:35   Home of Hezrai, one of David's mighty men
1 Chr 11:27   Home of Hezro, one of David's mighty men
2 Chr 26:10   King Uzziah had vineyards here
» It has been identified as present-day Khirbet el-Kermel, about 13 km south of Hebron. This is a tough one! The roads are paved but in terrible disrepair, and they seem to twist and turn in every direction. And you should be cautioned that the people in this general region are intensely anti-Israeli. Get to Yatta from the Hebron-Beersheva road along route #3266. On entering Yatta you will first of all come to a T-junction; take left (actually, the main road goes to the left anyway). Drive for less than 1 km to a Y-junction;

take left. After another 1 km, or a little less, the road takes a sharp left around the corner of a mosque. Within 100m there is a junction, sharp right and downhill. Take that and drive for about 7 km east on route #3267. If you get lost in Yatta, or when you get lost in Yatta, ask for directions to today's Arab village of Karmel. It is imperative that you make it abundantly clear that you are seeking for Khirbet Karmel, not the Jewish settlement of Karmel which is nearby. When you finally enter the village of Karmel, (map 10) turn right and drive for about 300m. The relatively scant ruins are about 100m off to the left and you will spot them in the spaces between the houses. Your next stop, Maon, is on top of the hill directly south from here.

MAON

In Judah (Jos 15:55)
'dwelling'
(Map 10)

1 Sam 25:2   Home of Nabal, husband of Abigail
1 Sam 23:24-28   David and his men encamp while fleeing
                   from Saul

» A city about 2 km south of Carmel, identified with Khirbet Main (locals pronounce it as 'mine'). Leave the ruins at Karmel and follow the very rough dirt road to the south for about 1.5 km. An even rougher road goes off to the left and traces it's way, for about 1 km, to the top of the hill on your left. Follow map 10.

DEBIR

In Judah (Jos 15:15), then given to the Levites (Jos 21:15)

Jos 10:38-40   Joshua captured Debir and killed its king
Jos 11:21,22   Joshua expelled the Anakites
Jos 15:15-17   Judge Othniel, younger brother of Caleb,
                   captured the city (Also Judg 1:11-13)
Jos 15:19   Caleb gave his daughter two springs
Judg 1:15   Caleb gave his daughter two springs

» There are two main contenders for the site of Debir. Formerly Kirjath-Sepher (Jos 15:15; Judg 1:11), also called Kirjath-Sannah (Jos 15:49). The first is identified as Tel Beit Mirsim and is about 20 km southwest of Hebron, near the village of El-Burj. Drive south

from Hebron on route #60 to Dhahiriya. As you are leaving the southern end of the town, turn right on route #354 and drive for about 7 km to the second turn to the left which goes to the village of El-Burj. Less than 2 km beyond this turnoff, still on route #354, you will come to a well-traveled dirt (gravel) road which leads to the very small village of Beit Mirsim about 1.5 km along (not marked on most maps). Ask the villagers to point the Tel to you and how to walk to it. The second, and the most likely site, is Tel Rabud, 12 km south of Hebron on route #60 on the southeast corner of the junction with route #356. This is actually a 4-way junction. Take the narrow road to the southeast for about 1 km until it ends. Rabud is the large hill directly in front of you. It's a tough, and unnecessary, walk to the top. Note that in Hebrew the consonant spelling if Debir is DBR and Rabud is RBD, which is Debir spelled backwards. The ancient Biblical name may have been preserved in this way.

Today there are many wells in the Rabud area, but only two of them are old. These are in the village about 2.5 km north of Rabud. One is clearly seen on the right-hand side of the road as you come near the village, and the other is up in the village. These might be the upper and lower wells that Caleb gave to his daughter when she complained about the aridity of the land she had been given.

EASTWARD FROM JERUSALEM

"The lot of the children of Joseph fell from Jordan by Jericho, unto the water of Jericho on the east"
Jos 16:1

JUDEAN DESERT

This is the desert between the Judean Hills (the central spine of mountains running north-south through the country) and the Dead Sea. Jewish rabbis have identified Mt. Azazel (Hebrew for 'the goat of removal') where the scapegoat was thrown over the edge of a cliff; Leviticus does not indicate that the goat was killed.

Lev 16:5-22   The scapegoat released to the wilderness
Mt 4:1-4   Jesus tempted in the desert

ADUMMIM

Part of the steep road between Jerusalem and Jericho traditionally assumed to be in the vicinity of the so-called "Inn of the Good Samaritan". While the Samaritan was evidently a "good" man, the Bible never gives him that title. The road is on the border of Judah and Benjamin (Jos 15:7; 18:17).

Lk 10:25-37   Parable of the "Good" Samaritan
» Follow route #1 between Jerusalem and Jericho.

VALLEY OF ACHOR

This is sometimes identified with el-Buqeia, a broad valley in the Judean desert. However, this in an unlikely identification because the Valley of Achor is on the northern border of Benjamin and south of Gilgal (Jos 15:7). It is more commonly identified as Wadi Kelt, a gorge running for about 12 km from Jericho to the west and readily accessible from the Jerusalem to Jericho road. Along Wadi Kelt, about 6 km before reaching Jericho, is St. George's monastery, a site commemorating the location of the attack in the story of the Good Samaritan (see also Adummim entry). As you drive along this road you will see a prominent cross to the north of the road about 1 km west of the monastery. From this cross you are offered a beautiful view of the monastery.

Jos 7:24-26   Achan and his family stoned, and burned
Lk 10:25-37   Parable of the "Good" Samaritan

» This is not exactly a Bible site, but the 4 hour hike along Wadi Kelt, passed the monastery, and on to Jericho, is one of the most beautiful in all Israel. Take a sherut (shared taxi) from Damascus Gate in Jerusalem and ask them to drop you of at Wadi Kelt. I don't have space to give all the detailed directions but any good Travel Guide will give you the necessary details.

JERICHO

In Benjamin (Jos 18:21)

(Map 12). Jericho was the first city captured by the Israelites under Joshua. It is about 27 km east of Jerusalem and 8 km west of the River Jordan. Being 250m below sea level, makes it the world's lowest town. The ancient town, Tel es-Sultan, lies on the northern outskirts of today's Arab town. The oldest remains are dated at 6000-8000 BC also making it the world's oldest city. Jericho is called the 'City of Palm Trees' (Deut 34:3; Judg 1:16; Judg 3:13; 2 Chr 28:15). Immediately beside the ancient Tel is the Spring of Elisha (Ein es-Sultan), and in the modern town some locals will show you a tree they claim was climbed by Zacchaeus when he wanted to see Jesus. The site of New Testament Jericho is largely dominated by the ruins of one of Herod's winter palaces. It was to here that he came during his last illness and where he died.

Jos 2:1-21	Home of Rahab the harlot
Jos 3:14-17	Israel crossed over the Jordan nearby
Jos 5:13-6:27	The battle and fall of Jericho
1 Ki 16:34	Hiel the Bethelite built Jericho
2 Ki 2:4-5	Elijah and Elisha went to Jericho
2 Ki 2:11-12	Elijah taken up to Heaven beside Jericho
2 Ki 2:19-22	Elisha purified the water with salt
Mt 20:29-34	Two blind men received sight
Mk 10:46-52	Jesus gives blind Bartimaeus his sight
Lk 18:35-43	Blind man received his sight
Lk 19:1-10	Zacchaeus and the sycamore tree

» There are three different Jerichos: New Testament Jericho which is about 2 km west of today's modern city which in turn is about   2 km from Old Testament Jericho.   The extensive ruins of one of Herod's

winter palaces are at the site of New Testament Jericho and are located just as the Wadi Kelt leaves the gorge and enters the flatland. Alternatively, drive into Jericho from Jerusalem until you see the mosque on your right. At the mosque, turn left of the main road and follow map 12.

MOUNT OF TEMPTATION

Overlooking Jericho, this mountain is traditionally associated with two of the temptations of the Lord Jesus. Matthew and Luke list the temptations in a different order. Inside the monastery the priests will show you a small chapel built over the traditional cave where Christ stayed during his 40 days temptation.

Mt 4:1-4	The first temptation of Jesus
Mt 4:8-11	The third temptation of Jesus
Mk 1:12	The temptation of Jesus
Lk 4:1-8	The first and second temptations of Jesus

» About 3 km northwest of Jericho and directly behind, and above, the ancient Tel. About one third way up the cliff a Greek Orthodox monastery clings to the side of the mount. Drive the short distance from the Tel, along the road to Ramallah (route #3), until you come to the car park. It is about a 15 minute hike to the monastery. For a small fee the priest will allow you to pass through the monastery and to climb for another 20mins to the top of the mount. The view over Jericho, the Jordan Valley, the Dead Sea and beyond is well worth the climb - and it is a great visual reminder of Jesus' third temptation (Mt 4:8-11).

GILGAL

'stone circle'

"God forbid that I should sin against the LORD in ceasing to pray for you" (1 Sam 12:23)

The first place the Children of Israel encamped after crossing the River Jordan. Despite its importance, the true site of Gilgal was, for a long time, lost. There were at least three main candidates. Gilgal is "in the east border of Jericho" (Jos 4:19), and is also called Gibeath Haaraloth, meaning 'hill of the foreskins' (Jos 5:3). Josephus says that it is "ten stadia (a stadia is about 185m) from Jericho", Eusebias locates it "at about the second milestone from Jericho" thus making Khirbet el-Mefjir as a possible location of this place.

Jos 4	Israel took 12 stones from the Jordan and built a memorial
Jos 4:19-5:12	The Israelites encamped
Jos 5:1-3	Israelites circumcised
Jos 5:9,10	Israelites celebrated first Passover in Canaan
Jos 5:13-15	Joshua met commander of the Lord's army
Jos 6	Israel encamped while taking Jericho
Jos 9:6-15	Israel made a treaty with the Gibeonites
Jos 10:6-9	Joshua's army fought for the Gibeonites
Jos 14:6	Joshua's headquarters
Judg 3:12-26	Judge Ehud murdered Eglon king of Moab
1 Sam 7:16-17	On Samuel's circuit as a judge of Israel
1 Sam 11:12-15	Saul confirmed as king
1 Sam 13:8-14	Saul made an unauthorized sacrifice
1 Sam 15:33	Samuel killed Agag, king of the Amalekites
2 Ki 4:38-41	Elisha cured the death in the pot

» One of the most confusing things about the search for ancient Gilgal is the number of conflicting theories. Gilgal is often identified with the ruins of Khirbet el-Mefjir, 2 km northeast of Jericho, and now occupied by the ruins of Hisham's palace. A second possible location is Tel Jaljul about 8 km north of Jericho; the Arab names preserves the Biblical name. Another theory places Gilgal just southeast of the Israelites traditional crossing point over the Jordan, about 9 km southeast of Jericho on the banks of the Jordan River - near the site of an ancient Greek Orthodox monastery called Qasr Al Yehud (see Bethabara entry below). A rather recent find about 0.7 km north of the monastery of Qasr Al Yehud, immediately to the east of the by-pass road, may be ancient Gilgal.

BETHABARA

'house of the ford'
This is close by the traditional place of Jesus' baptism. The exact location of 'Bethany beyond Jordan' is not certain but perhaps the most likely location is the Greek Orthodox monastery at Qasr Al Yehud (see previous entry).
Jn 1:28   John preached and baptized
» The site is not really accessible. However, one day per year, on the third Thursday of October, Christ's traditional baptismal site on the River Jordan is open to the public (current information can be obtained from the Christian Information Center just inside the Jaffa Gate in the Old City of Jerusalem). There are rumors that the baptismal site is being developed so as to be opened permanently as a pilgrimage site. If you can get to the baptismal site on this day you will pass within a few hundred meters of the old monastery which is about 1.5 km before the river.

"Lot lifted up his eyes and beheld all the
Plain of Jordan" (Gen 13:10).

RIVER JORDAN

"My father, my father, the chariot of Israel, and
the horsemen thereof." (2 Ki 2:12)

The River Jordan is mentioned 181 times in the Old testament and 15 times in the New Testament. It is the main river in Israel and flows from the Mt. Hermon region, through the Huleh, the Sea of Galilee to the Dead Sea. It has three major sources: the River Dan which issues from Dan Springs at Tel Dan (arab. Tel el-Qadi), the River Hermon from Banias Springs (Biblical Caesarea Philippi), and from just inside the Lebanese border (a mediaeval map calls it the River Jor). The Jordan is about 320 km long and for most of its length is below sea level. It winds for 167 km from the Sea of Galilee to the Dead Sea even though the distance is only 104 km. The name 'Jordan' means 'The Descender', or it may be named by combining the names of the Rivers Jor and Dan. It has been suggested that it is called the Jordan (Y-R-D-N) because it descends (Y-R-D) from Dan (D-N).

Jos 3:14-17	Children of Israel crossed opposite Jericho
2 Ki 2:8-9	Elijah divided the waters of the Jordan
2 Ki 2:11-12	Elijah taken up to Heaven
2 Ki 2:13,14	Elisha divided the Jordan with Elijah's cloak
2 Ki 5	Naaman the leper cured
2 Ki 6:1-7	Elisha made the axe head float
Mt 3:6; Mk 1:15	John baptized the people
Mt 3:13-17	Baptism of Jesus
	Also: Mk 1:9-11; Lk 3:21-22

ADAM BRIDGE
Named after the Biblical city of Adam, which is identified with Tel Damiya just over the border in Jordan (see Jordan entry; Map 29).

ZARETAN
Also spelled Zarethan (NIV), Zartanah (1 Ki 4:12) and Zeredathan (2 Chr 4:17). It is described as being by Beth Shean and by Adam (Jos 3:16) which themselves are 48 km apart. It's location has therefore been long debated.

» Most scholars suggest that this is Tel al-Saidiya. You may be able to get to it from the Jordanian side but we have never tried to do this. It is easily viewed from the Israeli side - but no photographs because you are in a military area. Traveling north on route #90 from Jericho, measure exactly 17 km from Adam junction. Or travel south from Beth Shean, it is 14 km south of Mehola junction. It is one of the most prominent mounds in the Jordan valley and you will see it long before you reach it from either direction.

CHERITH BROOK
'gorge, trench'
Most authorities identify Cherith as Wadi Yabis, east of the River Jordan opposite a point about 12 km south of Beth Shean. The Greek Orthodox identify it as the Wadi Kelt

immediately west of Jericho.

1 Ki 17:3-6   Elijah fed by ravens

DEAD SEA

Also known as the 'Vale of Siddim' (Gen 14:3), 'Salt Sea' the 'Arabah Sea' (Gen 14:3; Deut 3:17; Jos 3:16; 2 Ki 14:25) and the 'East Sea' (Ezk 47:18; Joel 2:20). It formed the eastern boundary of ancient Israel (2 Ki 14:25; Amos 6:14). Its shores are the lowest land point (-412m) on the earth's surface, and the deepest parts of the water are an additional 390m. It is approximately 80 km long and 15 km wide. During approximately the last 100 years the sea level has dropped about 12m. The western shore of the Dead Sea offers a scenic drive from Qumran to Sedom.

Gen 14:3-10   Kings warred against each other and
                against Chedorlaomer
Ezek 47:1-12   The river from the temple to the Dead Sea

»Drive north from En Gedi for about 16 km, or south from Qumran for about 25 km. Follow the signpost to Metzoke Dragot; the road turns to the west up to the top of the cliffs overlooking the Dead Sea. After 4.6 km and just before Metzoke Dragot, turn left into the parking lot for an awesome view of the Dead Sea.

QUMRAN

Many scholars identify this as the 'City of Salt' (Jos 15:62). In 1947, Bedouin shepherds found the Dead Sea Scrolls in caves close by the ruins of the ancient settlement. The Caves were numbered in the order in which they were found, so the first cave found was #1. Cave 1 contained the Isaiah A and Isaiah B Scrolls, a commentary on Habakkuk, and the 'Manual of Discipline'. Cave 3 produced the 'Copper Scroll', and Cave 4 produced the greatest finds with about 15000 different fragments including the "Acts of Torah'. Cave 11 contained the Psalms Scroll and parts of Leviticus and Ezekiel. The Psalms Scroll contains 38 Psalms from our Bible, in addition it included seven Apocryphal Psalms, three of which were not previously known (see panel). It also provided the "missing" verse 14 from

Psalm 145. Psalm 145 is an acrostic Psalm with each verse beginning with the next letter of the Hebrew alphabet, so scholars have always known that verse 14 was missing. It has now been inserted in the NIV as an extended verse 13 (compare vs. 13 in the King James and NIV). Cave 11 also contained 'The Temple Scroll', which is an Aramaic translation of a large portion of Job. Many of the scrolls are on display at the Shrine of the Book, Israel Museum, Jerusalem.

» *Qumran is on a small hill overlooking the northwest shore of the Dead Sea and about 13 km south of Jericho. You should make the effort to visit some of the caves. Cave 4 is viewed by all visitors to the ruins. Cave 6 (which didn't produce much of significance) is quite high on the cliff behind the settlement (and slightly to the left) and affords a great view of the entire site.*

JOSHUA'S SIX CITIES

Jos 15:20, 61-62 refers to six cities in the tribal allotment to Judah - Beth Arabah, Middin, Secacah, Nibshan, the City of Salt and Ein Gedi. Driving from the south you will first of all come to Ein Gedi. About 16 km north there is a turn off to the settlement of Metzoke Dragot. Keeping on the coastal road (route # 90) drive for 3.4 km to the City of Salt (Ein el-Turaba). The scant remains are about 80m of the road to the west and are easily seen from the road. Drive a further 2.25 km to Nishban (Ein el-Ghuweir). There are only a few stones from a few walls here and you will spot them about 20m to the east of the road after you have driven past the vegetation of the nature reserve. Then drive for another 6.6 km to a much larger structure at Middin (Khirbet Mazin) which is easily spotted to the east of the road. It seems that Secacah should be identified as the Iron II remains of the settlement at Qumran, and we don't seem to know much about the whereabouts of Beth Arabah.

EN GEDI

In Judah (Jos 15:62)
'the fountain of the kid'
Also referred to as the wilderness of En Gedi (1 Sam 24:10)
and as Hazazon-tamar (2 Chr 20:2).
Gen 14:7   Chedorlaomer conquered Amorites
1 Sam 23:29;24 David hid and spared Saul's life
Song 1:14   My lover is like .. vineyards of En Gedi
Ezek 47:10   Fish will return to the Dead Sea
» This is a small spring to the west of the Dead Sea 16 km north of
Masada on route #90. The synagogue at En Gedi is worth visiting.
The mosaic floor of the synagogue has an inscription giving the
genealogy of Japeth back to Adam (Gen 5).

MASADA

According to the Moody Bible Atlas, this may be David's hold
or stronghold.
1 Sam 22:4   King David at Masada
1 Sam 24:22   David rested while Saul searched for him

SODOM AND GOMORRAH

'place of lime' and 'submersion'
The exact location of these two cities is not known but there
are many speculations. Many scholars believe the cities may
be located beneath the shallow southern basin of the Dead
Sea. The name Sodom is today continued as Sedom on the
southern shores of the Dead Sea. The most accepted
locations are those of Bab Edh-Dhra and Numeira in Jordan,
opposite Masada (see Jordan entry; Map 26).

WESTWARD FROM JERUSALEM

BETH HORON UPPER AND BETH HORON LOWER

In Ephraim (Jos 16:3,5) and given to the Kohathites (Jos 21:20-22)

'house of hollowness'

(Map 3). Twin towns (today's Beit Ur el-Foka and Beit Ur et-Tahta) situated on the boundary between Benjamin and Ephraim, called Upper and Lower because of their difference in elevation (615 and 369 meters above sea level). The steep descent between them provided the best pass through the mountains from Jerusalem to Joppa (modern Jaffa) and the Mediterranean Sea.

Jos 10:10,11	Joshua pursued the Amorites
1 Sam 13:18	Philistines sent a raiding party from Michmash
1 Ki 9:17	Solomon rebuilt Lower Beth Horon
1 Chr 7:24	Beriah's daughter, Sheerah, rebuilt Lower and Upper Beth Horon
2 Chr 8:5	Solomon fortified Upper and Lower Beth Horon
Neh 2:10	Home of Sanballat

» Both villages, and the steep pass between them, are just to the north of route #3 between Ramallah and Latrun Interchange. About 3 km north of the prophet Samuel's tomb, route #437 meets route #3. Drive west on route #3 for 4.4 km and leave the main highway when you see the signpost for the Jewish settlement of Beit Horon. Beit Ur el-Foka is the next village past the settlement, and Beit Ur el-Tahta follows about 3 km further.

EMMAUS

(Map 3)

Mk 16:12-12	The two on the road to Emmaus
Lk 24:13-25	The two on the road to Emmaus

» Emmaus is about three score furlongs (Lk 24:13; just over 11 km) from Jerusalem. Four different modern towns have been proposed as being Emmaus (Abu Gosh, Qubeibeh, Amwas, and Motza). The one most often visited is today's village of Amwas, at the Latrun

*interchange, about 23 km from Jerusalem on the main highway to Tel
Aviv; there was an Emmaus here in Roman times, and an Imwas until
1967, but it is unlikely to be the Emmaus of Luke 24 because the
distance from Jerusalem is more than twice that given in the Biblical
narrative. The most likely site is Qubeibeh near the prophet Samuel's
tomb at Ramah about 11 km from Jerusalem. Travel north on route
#436 for about 2 km beyond Samuel's tomb. You will see a signpost
to the settlement of Givon Hahadasha. Drive the short distance to
Givon Hahadasha and continue beyond it for about 4 km to
Qubeibeh. On entering the village there is a 3-way intersection.
Turn right and the church is about 300m down the hill on your right.
The priest will show you some supposed remains of the house of
Cleopas (Lk 24:18).*

AIJALON

In Dan (Jos 19:42) and assigned to the Kohathite Levites (Jos
21:24)
'place of deer'
(Map 15). The main Jerusalem to Tel Aviv highway cuts across
the valley of Aijalon just west of the Judean Hills and
approaching the coastal plain. The very scant ruins of the city
of Aijalon are inside Canada Park.

Jos 10:12-14	Joshua prayed for the moon to stand still
2 Chr 11:10	City fortified by Rehoboam
2 Chr 28:18	Captured by the Philistines in the days of Ahaz

*»The city of Aijalon is identified as Khirbet Haiyan about 26 km
northwest of Jerusalem. The ruins are in Ayalon forest inside Canada
Park the entrance to which is about 1 km north of Emmaus at the
Latrun interchange (see map 15). There are three roads at the
entrance of Canada Park but all end up at the same place. Take the
middle (main) of the three roads and continue for about 2 km over an
animal grid and bear to the left at the next junction. Within 100m is
a beautiful viewpoint over the Aijalon valley and the site of the city is
on the top of the mound at your far right. Drive for a further 1.6 km
to the totally uninspiring mound.*

EIN KEREM

Formerly identified as Bet Hakkerem but this has long been rejected.
Church of the Visitation
Lk 1:39-56   Mary visited Elizabeth; the Magnificat

Church of St. John
Lk 1:57-58   Birth of John the Baptist
»A village about 8 km west of Jerusalem on 'the old road' to Tel Aviv.

KING HEZEKIAH'S BURIAL MEMORIAL

West of Jerusalem are a group of about 20 tumuli, or mounds, which are a puzzle for archeologists. It has been proposed that these are memorials to the kings of Judah. If so, then one of the larger mounds may belong to king Hezekiah, one of the greatest of the Judean kings.
»Drive out of Jerusalem along Hertzl Blvd. following signs to Ein Kerem or the Hadassah Medical Center. Immediately beyond Yad Vashem you will not miss the ugly red sculpture where the road branches off to the right to Ein Kerem. Drive straight on towards Hadassah Medical Center for exactly 5 km until you see Panama St. to the left. This is about 50m before an intersection with roads leading to Hadassah and to Ora. Drive up Panama St. for 0.5 km until the Schever-Grassler Community Center on the right. Park here and walk. You will see the main tumulus about 100 m behind the Community Center, and there are 4 or 5 others in the immediate area.

KIRIATH JEARIM

In Judah (Jos 15:60) then Benjamin (Jos 18:14)
'city of forests'
Also called Kiriath Baal (Jos 15:60), Baalah (Jos 15:9), Baale Judah (2 Sam 6:2), and Kiriath (Jos 18:28).
Judg 18:11,12   Danites camped on their way to settle Laish
1 Sam 6:21-7:1   Ark brought here from Beth Shemesh
1 Sam 7:1   Ark kept by Eleazar at Abinadab's house
1 Sam 7:2   Ark of God stayed for twenty years

2 Sam 6	David brought the ark to Jerusalem
1 Chr 13:5-8	David brought the ark to Jerusalem
Neh 7:5,6,29	Some of the people who returned from captivity in Babylon

» Today's village of Abu Gosh, about 13 km from Jerusalem on the road to Tel Aviv. The location you are looking for has an enormous statue of the virgin Mary atop the church of Notre Dame de l'Arche d'Alliance.

ZORAH AND ESHTAOL

In Dan (Jos 19:41)
'place of hornets'
(Map 13). Zorah is often mentioned together with Eshtaol which is about 3 km to the north.

Judg 13:2-5,24	Birthplace of Samson
Judg 16:31	Samson buried nearby
2 Chr 11:10	Zorah fortified by Rehoboam

» Zorah is 29 km west of Jerusalem, on route #38, on a hill above the Valley of Sorek.

ALTAR OF MANOAH

(Map 16). This is a rock altar built as the Hebrews would have built an altar in the time of the judges. Many authorities believe that this could be the altar where Manoah presented his offering.

| Judg 13:15-23 | Angel of the Lord appeared to Manoah |

» Drive 1 km south of Shimshon (Hebrew for Samson) junction on route #38 towards Beth Shemesh. Follow the sign to the right to 'Industry' and follow map 16. When you park, climb up the slope opposite and start your search. There are innumerable large rocks but keep to the south and to the west of these and circle clockwise. The altar used to be recognizable by having a tree growing from it - then some delinquent cut it down. The altar then had some graffiti. A subsequent visit in 1997 revealed an increasing mess; a new road was being constructed through the location and the altar had been unceremonially dumped (still the correct way up!) among all the other debris resulting from the road clearing activities. Then in

1998, I couldn't find the altar at all and I have no idea where it is.

BROOK OF SOREK
(Map 13)

Judg 16:4-21   Samson and Delilah
Judg 16:21   Samson's eyes gouged out

» The easiest place to view the brook is on the northern outskirts of Beth Shemesh, or follow the road to kibbutz Zorah.

BETH SHEMESH

In Judah (Jos 15:10), then Dan (Jos 19:41), then given to the Levites (Jos 21:16). It was a major Canaanite city-state and then an Israelite royal administrative center.
'house of the sun'
(Map 13)

1 Sam 6:9-18   The ark of God came from Ekron
1 Sam 6:19   Seventy men killed for looking into the ark
2 Ki 14:11-14   Jehoash defeated Amaziah
2 Chr 25:21-23 Jehoash and Amaziah in battle
2 Chr 28:18   Philistines captured the city

» About 26 km west of Jerusalem overlooking the Valley of the Brook Sorek. It is 5 km south of the Sha'ar Hagai junction on route #38. The road crosses the railway, proceeds past modern Beth Shemesh on the left, and than climbs up a hill. The ruins are at the top of the hill just to the right of the road.

TIMNAH

In Dan (Jos 19:43)
'allotted portion'
(Maps 13&14). Also called Timnath (Gen 38:13), now identified as Tel Batash. Also called Thimnathah (Jos 19:43).

Judg 14:1-3   Samson found his wife
Judg 14:5-6   Samson killed a young lion
2 Chr 28:18   Philistines captured the city

» Access is quite difficult but can be gained by following the 'road' alongside the Brook Sorek for about 6 km from Beth Shemesh. This road passes modern kibbutz Zorah, but unfortunately the Brook

Sorek is always between you and the Tel. Alternatively, drive the dirt tracks through and beyond the kibbutz at Tal Sharar (about 2 km west of Nashon junct. on route #3). From the main road, drive 0.8 km into the settlement to a sharp bend in the road; a rough road goes straight ahead at this point. Take this road for 2.7 km over the Brook Sorek to the railway. When the road reaches the railway you have two choices. If the season is wet, cross over the railway and immediately turn left, drive for 1.4 km and view the Tel from a distance. If the season is dry, keep to the north side of the railway and follow map 14. You will most likely have to walk the final few hundred meters.

BEIT JIMAL

(Maps 13 & 17). This is the site of the Jewish village of Gamala, birthplace of Rabban Gamaliel, head of the Sanhedrin, who, according to tradition, defended Stephen the first Christian martyr. It may also be the site of En-Gannim (Jos 15:34). The site has a monastery behind which is a pretty little church painted in mock Byzantine, and which has four beautiful murals depicting the commissioning, trial, stoning, and burial of Stephen. The mural showing the stoning of Stephen also shows Saul, later Paul, holding the garments of the witnesses (Acts 7:58; 22:20). There is a tradition that the body of Stephen was discovered here in 415AD and the body was taken to Jerusalem and interred where the Church of the Dormition now stands, on Mt. Zion.

Acts 5:33-41   Apostles before the Sanhedrin
Acts 6:12   Stephen before the Sanhedrin
Acts 22:2,3   Gamaliel was Paul's teacher*

* It is early Christian tradition that Gamaliel was also Stephen's teacher.

» A well-signposted monastery about 2 km south of Beth Shemesh east of the road to Beit Guvrin.

MAKKEDAH

In Judah (Jos 15:41)
'place of shepherds'
Makkedah refers to both a cave and to a city. This is a particularly difficult one. The major story connected with this location takes place in a cave near the city - this whole region is riddled with caves - so the location is uncertain. One popularly cited location is Khirbet el-Kum (Khirbet el-Oom) or Khirbet Beit Maqdum about 14 km west of Hebron towards Beit Guvrin - we never even tried to find this one. Another possible location is Khirbet el-Kheishum northeast of Azekah.

Jos 10:10	Joshua pursued Amorite kings
Jos 10:16, 17	Five Amorite kings hid in a cave
Jos 10:22-27	Five kings killed and put in cave
Jos 10:28	Joshua captured the city and killed its king (also Jos 12:16)

» Drive south from Beth Shemesh, 1.3 km south of the junction to Beit Jimal, and about 200m before the junction to Ramat Bet Shemesh. A narrow gravel road takes off to the west. It is rough but quite well graded. After 0.5 km you arrive at a square parking area but keep going straight. After a further 0.5 km you reach a large triangular area; turn right for 0.35 km to the top of the hill at a T-junction. The area you are looking for (Hurbat Husham) is that rather uninspiring place behind the fence with all the military signs! Best not go in, even though it looks like a very long time since the military have been there.

JARMUTH

In Judah (Jos 15:35)
(Maps 13 & 17). There was also a Jarmuth in Issachar (Jos 21:29) tentatively identified with the site of Belvoir castle.

Jos 10:3-5	Piram king of Jarmuth was one of the five Amorite kings
Jos 10:16-27	Joshua killed the King of Jarmuth
Neh 11:29	Inhabited by the returned exiles of Judah

» Tel Yarmut is about 5 km south of Beth Shemesh on the east side of the road (route #38) that leads to Beit Guvrin. About 3.4 km south of Beth Shemesh leave the main road following the sign to Ramat Bet Shemesh. Follow this road for 0.9 km (to where the power lines cross the road), park, and walk the remaining 0.7 km to the top of the Tel (see map 17).

AZEKAH
In Judah (Jos 15:35)
'a place tilled'
(Map 13). Overlooks the Valley of Elah.

Jos 10:10	Joshua defeated the five Canaanite kings
Jos 10:11	Troops of five Canaanite kings killed with hailstones
Jer 34:6,7	Nebuchadnezzar attacked the city

» About 8 km south of Beth Shemesh on route #38. The hill of Azekah is immediately southwest of the junction with route #383.

ELAH VALLEY
(Map 13). Scripture indicates that the Philistines encamped between Azekah and Socoh so the site of the battle is probably somewhere between the road and a few hundred meters upstream (1 Sam 17:1-4).

1 Sam 17	The battleground of David and Goliath

» About 1 km south of the junction with route #383, route #38 crosses a little brook which is mostly dried up.

SOCOH
In Judah (Jos 15:35)
'thornhedge'
(Map 13). There is also a Socoh near Debir (Jos 15:48) at Khirbet Shuweikeh 3 km east of Dhahiriya, and one in the Plain of Sharon (1 Ki 4:10).

1 Sam 17:1	Philistines gathered before battle with David
1 Sam 17:1	Philistines encamped nearby
2 Chr 28:18	Philistines captured the city

» Tel Sokho is 2.5 km east of Haela Junction on route #375. Turn off the road to the south and follow the dirt track for about 200m, park, and climb to the top of the Tel. In spring time, this tel has an amazing display of wildflowers, especially cyclamen and lupine.

ADULLAM

In Judah (Jos 15:35)
'refuge'
(Map 13)

Gen 38:1-10	Judah married Shua; two sons killed
Jos 12:15	Joshua killed the king of Adullam
2 Chr 11:5,7	Rehoboam fortified the city

» A city located in the Shephelah about 6 km east of the road half way between Beth Shemesh and Moresheth. Go east beyond Sokho (previous entry) about 0.9 km to a junction which has a signpost saying Adullam, via the settlement of Adderet. This one baffled us! According to most maps you can get to Adullam by going through either the settlement Adderet or through Newe Mikhael. It's easy to get to both of these settlements but, unfortunately, both have blocked their roads to through traffic.

MORESHETH

'possession'
(Map 13). Also Moresheth Gath (Mic 1:14).

Judg 15:15-19	Samson hid after killing 1000 Philistines
Jer 26:18	Micah of Moresheth
Mic 1:1	Birthplace of the prophet Micah

» Identified as Tel Goded (Tell Judeideh) about 18 km south of Beth Shemesh on the west side of route #38. Coming from Beit Guvrin to the south, leave route #35, turn north on route #38 and drive 2.4 km to a fairly obvious gate at a parking spot; the well-worn path leads straight to the top of the quite imposing mound. But if you are short of time, there's not much to see up there except for the view. But do take time to walk in through the gate. About 30m in front of you is a well which is the traditional location where Samson hid after killing the Philistines.

MARESHAH

In Judah (Jos 15:44)
'summit'
(Map 13)
2 Chr 11:5-12   Rehoboam fortified the city
2 Chr 14:9,10   King Asa (Judah) fought with Zerah the
                 Ethiopian
» Situated in the Beit Guvrin National Park.

LACHISH

In Judah (Jos 15:39)
(Map 13)
Jos 10:3,5,23   King was one of the five Canaanite kings
Jos 10:3-27   Joshua killed Japhia king of Lachish
Jos 10:31-33   Lachish defeated by Joshua
2 Ki 14:17-21   Amaziah king of Judah killed
2 Ki 18:13-15   Sennacherib attacked the city
2 Chr 11:5-12   Rehoboam fortified the city
2 Chr 25:27   Amaziah, king of Judah, killed here
Jer 34:6,7   Nebuchadnezzar attacked the city
» Situated just to the south of the road from Hebron to Kiryat Gat
(route #35), this was a vital trade routes in historic times. Lachish is
6 km west of Beit Guvrin on route #35, and 9.2 km east of the main
motorway (route #40). When you leave route #35 it is 3 km to the Tel.
This is one of the most prominent Tels in the region and you have to
stand on top to appreciate its commanding position..

GEZER

In Ephraim and given to the Levites (Jos 21:21), and a City of
Refuge (1 Chr 6:67)
'portion, division'
*(Map 18). Also called Gazer (1 Chr 14:16) and Gob (2 Sam
21:18). An ancient Canaanite city. Its chief attraction is the
High Place, a row of 10 monoliths dated to 1600BC, and
standing up to 3m tall. Also you will see an underground water
system dated to at least 1000BC. From the Tel Aviv to*

Jerusalem highway, Tel Gezer is rather unremarkable. Only when you stand atop the Tel can you appreciate its prominent view.

Jos 10:33	Conquered by Joshua
Judg 1:29	Canaanites dwelt in Gezer
2 Sam 5:25	David warred against the Philistines
2 Sam 21:19	Goliath the Gittite killed
1 Ki 9:16	Pharaoh king of Egypt captured the city and set it on fire
1 Ki 9:16	Pharaoh's daughter (Solomon's wife) given the city as a gift
1 Ki 9:15-19	Rebuilt by Solomon; a strategic military and economic center

» Gezer is 30 km west of Jerusalem on the road to Tel Aviv. There are two routes to the Tel at Gezer. Easiest is to follow route #44 north for 2.9 km from Nashon junction to the settlement of Karme Yosef. Follow map 18 to the barrier which is usually open until 5pm - but not on the Sabbath. If the barrier is locked, follow the map for the 10 minute walk, otherwise you can drive beyond the barrier - but return before 5pm! Alternatively you can approach through the settlement of Gezer on route #424. Initially there are signs to Tel Gezer, but once you have passed through the settlement you are on your own to decide how to best reach the Tel which is nearly always in view ahead of you and to the left. The only real decision, about 400m from the top, is to choose the left hand track when you come to a place where the road forks three ways.

GIBBETHON

In Dan (Jos 19:44) but given to the Levites (Jos 21:23)
'mound' or 'height'

1 Ki 15:27	Baasha killed Nadab king of Israel
	This was a Philistine city
1 Ki 16:15	Zimri king of Judah camped
1 Ki 16:16	Omri proclaimed king of Israel

» Today's Tel Malot beside the moshav Yaziz about 7 km west of Gezer. From Nashon junction drive west for 1.5 km; turn right and follow the sign to Rehovot for 8.5 km crossing two separate railway

tracks en route. Turn right for 0.5 km following the signs to Yaziz.
Opposite a row of small stores turn left for 0.6 km, then turn right and
drive for 2.4 km to the far end of Yaziz. When the good road takes a
left, you go straight on for another 250m to the railway tracks. Park
here and walk. The Tel is between the two tracks and about 350m to
your right. The easiest would be to walk along the tracks until you
reach the Tel on your left - but it is illegal to walk along the tracks.
Besides, there is absolutely nothing to see at this Tel anyway!

SHAALBIM

In Benjamin (Jos 19:42)
Also spelled Shaalabbin (Jos 19:42) and possibly Shaalbon (2
Sam 23:32; 1 Chr 11:33), it is a city near Mt. Heres and Aijalon
(Judg 1:35)

Judg 1:35	The Amorites lived here but were captured by the house of Joseph
1 Ki 4:9	Ben-Deker was the king's officer

» This is Tel Sha'alvim. Leave route #1 at the Latrun interchange
and follow signs towards Ramla. After about 5 km you will reach
Mishmar. Turn right and follow the signs for about 5 km to
Sha'alvim. When you enter the settlement carry straight on to the top
of the tel. There are some ruins to be seen but generally this Tel is
an overgrown mess. However, from the top of the Tel you have a
wonderful view of Gezer, Emmaus and the valley of Aijalon.

EKRON

In Judah (Jos 15:45) then Dan (Jos 19:43)
'barren place'
(Map 13). One of the five main cities of the Philistines.

1 Sam 5:10	Ark of God brought from Gath
1 Sam 17:52	After Goliath's death, Philistines pursued to Ekron
Judg 1:18	Men of Judah captured the city
2 Ki 1:3	Ahaziah consulted with Baal-Zebub, god of Ekron
Amos 1:8	Judgment on Ekron

» Now identified as Tel Miqne about 17 km west of Beth Shemesh following routes #44 and then #3. Access is gained via kibbutz Revadim 3 km north of the Re'em junction on route #3.

GATH

'wine press'

(Map 13). Gath was one of the five main cities of the Philistines.

Jos 11:22	Residence of the 'giant' Anakim
1 Sam 5:8-9	Ark of God brought from Ashdod
1 Sam 17:4	Goliath's home town
1 Sam 17:52	After Goliath's death, Philistines pursued to Gath
1 Sam 21:10-15	David escaped to Gath
1 Sam 27:3,4	David and his men settled in Gath
2 Sam 21:20	Residence of a huge man with six fingers and six toes
2 Ki 12:17	Hazael, king of Aram, captured Gath
1 Chr 18:1	David and his men captured Gath
2 Chr 26:5,6	King Uzziah broke down the walls of Gath

» Most likely this is Tel Tzafit (Tel es-Safi) about 10 km west of Azekah on route #383; some scholars identify this Tel as Biblical Libnah. Access is via the 3.5 km long road to the Tzafit Power Plant about 3 km east of Kibbutz Menahem. Gath was originally identified at two putative locations, but both claims have been abandoned. One was at Tel Nagila about 16 km south of Qiryat Gat to the west of route #40 (access by the Furna nature Reserve). The second was at Tel Erani on the northern outskirts of Qiryat Gat. The kibbutz Gat(h) is nearby.

LIBNAH

In Judah, reassigned to the Aaronites as a Levitical city (Jos 21:13;1 Chr 6:57).

'whiteness'

(Map 13). There are two Biblical sites with this name; one is the name of a campsite during the exodus (Num 33:20-21) and the other is a Canaanite city. Identification of the site is very

uncertain but some suggest that it may be Tel Tzafit (see Gath entry).

Jos 10:29,39	City captured by Joshua
2 Ki 8:22	Libnah revolted against Jehoram's authority
2 Ki 19:8	King of Assyria warred against Libnah
2 Ki 23:31	King Jehoahaz's grandfather was from Libnah
2 Ki 24:18	King Zedekiah's grandfather was from Libnah (also Jer 52:1)
2 Chr 21:10	Libnah revolted against Jehoram's authority

EGLON
'young bull'
(Map 19). Some identify it with Tel Beit Mirsim to the southwest of Hebron.

Jos 10:5,6,23	King of Eglon one of five Canaanite kings
Jos 10:3-27	Joshua killed Debir king of Eglon
Jos 10:34,35	Joshua captured the city

» Now identified as Tel Hasi about 35 km north of Beersheva on route #40. Can be a daunting one but actually quite easy. Drive south of Qiryat Gat on route #40, pass Uzza on the left and note the signpost to Etam to the right. Continue on route #40 for 1.3 km south of this sign and an inconspicuous dirt road takes off at right angles to the west. Follow map 19 for about 4 km to the Tel. Careful, this road can be washed out, especially in the springtime. Typically, you will reach the Nahal Shiqma but I don't advise you try to drive through it. Rather, park here, wade across the stream, and walk the remainder to the Tel.

ZIKLAG
In Judah (Jos 15:1,31) reallocated to the tribe of Simeon (Jos 19:5; 1 Chr. 4:30)
(Map 21)

Arise, walk through the land

1 Sam 27:5-7	Achish, king of Gath gave the city to David
1 Sam 27:8-12	David's military base for raids against people of the Negev
1 Sam 28:1,2	Achish appointed David bodyguard for life
1 Sam 30:1	Philistines burned the city
1 Sam 30:2	Philistines kidnapped the people, including David's two wives
1 Sam 30:3-25	David pursued the Philistines nearby
2 Sam 1:1	David returned after defeating the Amalekites
2 Sam 1:2-16	David heard of Saul's death
2 Sam 4:10	David killed the Amalekite who claimed to kill King Saul
1 Chr 12:1-22	Many of Saul's followers defected to David
Neh 11:28	Inhabited by the returned exiles of Judah

» The identification of Ziklag is not certain. It is possibly Tel es-Khuweilfeh (heb. Tel Halif), about 16 km northeast of Beersheva and about 8 km southwest of Tel Beit Mirsim (Debir), immediately beside kibbutz Lehav. From route #40 turn east on route #326 towards Lehav. After 8.6 km veer off to the right and drive towards the settlement. After 1 km the road turns quite sharply right and uphill. Park at the corner and the Tel is immediately above you and to your left (see Remmon). Ziklag may also be Tel esh-Shari'a (heb. Tel Shera) midway between Gaza and Beersheva and about 20 km from them. This Tel has been identified by some as Gath, Hormah and Gerar, but Ziklag is most commonly accepted. Leave route #40 at the Qama junction going west. After only a few hundred meters turn south following the signs to Shoval on route #264. When you reach the Shoval/Rahat junction, continue along #264 for 2.6 km. A dirt road to the right brings you to the Tel - follow Map 21. Be careful, this dirt track used to begin about 1 km south of Shoval but its entry point seems to change! Access to the Tel can also be achieved from the other direction, from route #25 near Berosh, but this is not advisable because there are too many opportunities to take a wrong turn! And then a final twist; at least one scholar places Ziklag at Tel es-Saba which is typically accepted as the site of ancient Beersheva.

REMMON
'pomegranate'
In Judah (Jos 15:32) and reallocated to the tribe of Simeon (Jos 19:7; 1Chr 4:32).
Also called En-rimmon (Neh 11:29).
Neh 11:29   Returning exiles lived here
Zec 14:10   Land will become desolate
» The identification of Remmon is not certain. It is possibly Tel Halif also described in the previous entry (see Ziklag).

GERAR
'halting place'
Biblically, it is between Kadesh and Shur (Gen 20:1).
Gen 20   Abraham lied to Abimelech about Sarah
Gen 26:1-6   Isaac went to Gerar
Gen 26:7-11   Isaac lied to Abimelech about Rebekah
Gen 26:12-22   Isaac's prosperity, and quarrels over wells
2 Chr 14:12-14 Asa and Judah plundered the Cushites
» Identified by some as Tel Abu Hureirah (heb. Tel Haror) 17 km southwest of Gaza, about halfway between Gaza and Beersheva on route #25. Drive south on route #25 for 3.3 km from Hagaddi junction. A rather inconspicuous track leaves the road to the right to a picnic area. Follow this track for about 1 km to the Tel. Other scholars identify it as Tel Gamma, near Re'im on the bank of Nahal Besor about 15 km south of Gaza on route #232. Drive south of Re'im junction for 0.5 km then turn right on to a paved but very narrow road and drive for 0.3 km to a parking spot. Occasionally Gerar has been identified as Tel Shera (see Ziklag entry).

BESOR BROOK
'cold'
A wadi, or dry river bed, south of Ziklag, passing Tel Gamma (possibly Biblical Gerar) entering the sea just south of Gaza.
1 Sam 30:9-21   David and 600 men pursued the Amalekites

Arise, walk through the land   91

NEGEV DESERT

"And Abram journeyed, going on still toward the south" (Gen 12:9).

NEGEV DESERT

'dry, parched'
A dry scrubland and desert from Beersheva to the south of Israel. It is the eastern extension of the Sinai and is described as "a land of hardship and distress' (Is 30:6). The two major locations of Biblical interest are the Wilderness of Zin and the Wilderness of Paran. Their exact boundaries cannot be determined. Paran may have been the general wilderness region of the central and southern Negev with Zin being a specific area within Paran. However, it is more generally assumed that the wilderness of Zin, sometimes referred to as the High Negev or the Central Negev, extended as far west as the area of Kadesh-Barnea and as far east as Edom. The southern Negev conforms approximately to the wilderness of Paran. The wilderness of Zin marked the southern boundary of ancient Israel (Num 34:3). Today, the name applies to a valley (really a canyon), that crosses the Negev about 40 km south of Beersheva, at Sede Boqer. The name Paran is today applied to one of the central valleys of the Negev about 50 km south of Mitzpeh Ramon.

Gen 12:9; 13:1	Abram travelled in the Negev
Num 13:17,22	Spies travelled through the Negev
Num 13:29	Amalekites lived there

WILDERNESS OF ZIN

Num 13:21	Part of the wilderness wanderings
Num 20:1	Miriam died and was buried here
Num 20:8-11	Moses struck the rock twice
Num 34:3	Southern boundary of ancient Israel

» To get the best view of the Wilderness of Zin, drive south on route #40 from Beersheva towards Eilat. After about 35-40 km you will come to kibbutz Sede Boqer. Drive beyond the kibbutz for another 3 km until you see the sign to the Ben Gurion burial grounds which are at the edge of the campus of the Blaustein Institute for Desert Research (the sign posts say Midreshet Sede Boqer, or Midreshet Ben Gurion). Drive the short distance to the graves and from this site

enjoy one of the most spectacular views in all of Israel. If you have the time, drive downhill from the graves to the nature reserve of En Avdat. This site has no biblical significance but when you are this close you don't want to miss it; climb the ladders to the top of the cliff and you will be rewarded by an even more spectacular view than that of the Wilderness of Zin. However, if you want to see this view point, and don't have the time to walk, there is an easier way. From the Ben Gurion graves drive back to the main road, turn south towards Eilat on route #40 for about 5 km, and follow the signs to En Avdat. The view point is only a few meters from the parking lot.

KADESH, KADESH BARNEA

'consecrated'

Called both Kadesh (Gen 14:7), Kadesh-Barnea (Jos 10:41); and En-mishpat (Gen 14:7). Kadesh Barnea is in the northeastern Sinai, an 11 day journey from Mt. Horeb (Deut 1:2) and in a wilderness area (Ps 29:8) between Egypt and Canaan. Here the children of Israel camped for about 38 years (compare Num 20:1 and Num 33:36-38) during the Exodus. Kadesh was apparently their headquarters during these years and in the 40th year the people again assembled at Kadesh for their final march to the Promised Land. Kadesh Barnea was situated on the edge of Edom (Num 20:16) and in the Wilderness of Paran (Num. 13:26). Paran was the general name for the wilderness region. Kadesh Barnea is usually identified with Ein el Gudeirat

Gen 14:7	Chedorlaomer defeated the Amalekites and Amorites
Gen 16:14	Abraham lived at wells nearby
Gen 20:1	Abraham lived nearby
Nub 13:1-16	Spies sent to explore the land
Num 13:26	Spies returned after viewing the land
Num 16:1-3	Rebellion against Moses and Aaron
Num 16:31, 32	Rebellion leaders killed by an earthquake
Num 20:1	The people of Israel lived in Kadesh
Num 20:1	Miriam died and was buried here
Num 20:8-11	Moses struck the rock twice

Num 20:13	Became known as the Water of Meribah
Num 33:36	On the route of the Exodus wanderings
Jos10:41	Joshua defeated Canaanites
Jos 15:3	City on the southern boundary of Palestine
Ezk 47:19	The southern boundary of the land
Ezk 48:28	The southern boundary of Gad

» I must confess I have no idea how to get to Kadesh Barnea. It is about 60 km from Beersheva in the Sinai desert (in Egypt) about 8 km from the Israeli border, just south of Nizzana. You can, however, get close. Drive south through the Negev desert from Beersheva along route #40. About 3 km before entering Mitzpeh Ramon take route #171 to the west and drive the 34 km to the Egyptian border. You will pass through at least one army control point along this road. When you reach the Egyptian border you are on your own - the road along the border is a military road that you can only use under special circumstances - and viewing Kadesh Barnea is not an acceptable reason! Nevertheless, if you can get on to this road, drive north along the border (route #10) for about 15 km. This is the closest you can get to Kadesh Barnea from the Israeli side; it is about 8 km due west from here in the Sinai.

WILDERNESS OF PARAN

The Paran is a vast barren land of sand and rock, with few means of survival.

| Gen 21:20-21 | Ishmael lived in wilderness of Paran |
| Num 12:16 | Israel camped in the wilderness of Paran |

» From Mitzpeh Ramon, keep driving south on route #40 for about 50 km until you come to Wadi Faran, or Wadi Paran. This fairly expansive plain stretches from the Arabah in the east and beyond the Egyptian border to the west.

TABERAH

Beer Ada has been tentatively identified as Biblical Taberah (50 km east of Har Karkom) by Professor Emmanuel Anati.

| Num 11:1-3 | Fire consumed the outskirts of the camp |
| Deut 9:22 | The people made the Lord angry |

» I can get there but I couldn't give you directions! It's only about 6 km to the west of the main road (route #40), along the Wadi Faran, but you definitely need a guide and a 4-wheel drive, or jeep.

HAR KARKOM
'Saffron Mountain'
One theory, not widely accepted among scholars, is that the real Mt. Sinai is Har Karkom located in the western Negev about 40 km southwest of Mitzpeh Ramon. It boasts 35000 petroglyphs which is the largest concentration of rock art in the Negev. This mountain is about 25 km west of the main road and is located at the western end of Paran - this is 4-wheel drive country and you definitely need a guide operating out of Mitzpeh Ramon. It is a large mesa-shaped mountain (847m high) in the western Paran, known to local Bedouins as Jebel Ideid; this is a peculiar name which may mean Mt. of the Multitude, Mt. of the Preparation, or Mt. of the Commemorations (See Mt. Sinai entry).

BEERSHEVA
Given to Judah (Jos 15:28) then to Simeon (Jos 19:1,2)
'well of seven' or 'well of the oath' (Gen 21:31).
Beersheva was the center of patriarchal life. Throughout Israel's settled history, it was recognized as the southern boundary of the country and there are at least ten Biblical references defining the country as stretching from Dan to Beersheva (e.g. Judg 20:1; 1 Sam 3:20; 1 Ki 4:25). At the site there are two significant displays - a great horned altar, and a well at the city gate. This deep well is dated to the 12th century BC. If dated correctly, this well was probably in use during the time of the patriarchs and may be the one at which Abraham and Abimelech made their oath (Beersheva means "the well of the oath") because it is at the city gate.

Gen 21:11-19	Hagar and Ishmael sent into the desert
Gen 21:25-33	Abraham and Abimelech's agreement
Gen 21:33	Abraham planted a tamarisk tree

Arise, walk through the land

Gen 22:19	Abraham lived in Beersheva
Gen 26:23-25	Isaac built an altar and dug a well
Gen 46:1-5	God told Jacob (Israel) to go to Egypt
1 Sam 8:2	Samuel's two sons were judges here
1 Ki 19:1-3	Elijah took refuge from Ahab and Jezebel
2 Chr 30:5	From Dan to Beersheva (see Dan)

» Ancient Beersheva is Tel es-Saba about 4 km east of the modern city on route #60 to Hebron.

BETH PELET

In Judah (Jos 15:27)
'house of escape'
(Map 11). The King James calls it Beth-palet (Jos 15:27) and Beth-phelet (Neh 11:26).

| Neh 11:26 | Some people of Judah lived here |

» See the directions to Hormah below; about 1 km before leaving the highway to cross the railway, on the outside of the large sweeping bend, at the foot of the hill is the possible site of Biblical Beth Pelet. What ruins there were (Hurbat Mizbah) seem to have been demolished, destroyed, stolen, or covered by Bedouin dwellings.

HORMAH

Allotted to Simeon (Jos 19:4) but within the territory of Judah (Jos 15:30).
'complete destruction'
(Map 11). Originally called Zephath, the name was changed when it was captured by Judah and Simeon and completely destroyed (Judg 1:17).

Num 14:39-45	Amalekites and the Canaanites defeated people of Israel
Num 21:1-3	Israelites destroyed the Canaanites
Deut 1:44	Amorites destroyed the Israelites
Jos12:14	City captured by Joshua
Judg 1:17	Captured by Judah and Simeon
1 Sam 30:26-30	David distributed the spoils of Hormah

» Identified as Tel Masos (Tel Mashosh). Drive 15.5 km east of Beersheva on route #25 towards Dimona. The highway takes a wide sweeping S-bend, first moving away from the railway and then moving close beside it again. Leave the highway at this point, cross the railroad and follow map 11.

AROER
'ruins' or 'crest of a mountain'
(Map 11). This may be the Adadah of Jos 15:22. There are two other towns in the Old Testament with this name; one on the northern bank of the Arnon River (see section on Jordan), and one in Gilead situated east of Rabbah in the territory of Gad (Num 32:34) but its exact location is not known.
1 Sam 30:26-31   David sent gifts to some elders
» See the directions to Hormah above. Instead of leaving route #25 to cross the railway, continue east for another 5 km, to within about 1 km of the junction with route #80 to Arad. The high mound (Khirbet Ar'areh) is very conspicuous to the south. Drive 0.3 km almost to the top of the mound.

ARAD
'fugitive'
Num 21:1-3   The king of Arad defeated
Jos 12:14   Joshua defeated the king of Arad
» In the northeastern Negev about 34 km east of Beersheva on route #31, and south of Hebron. The ancient Tel is 10 km west of today's city of Arad.

DIBON
Dibon was in southern Judah near the boundary of Edom. Also called Dimonah (Jos 15:22). There was also a Dibon in Moab just north of the Arnon gorge (see Dibon entry in Jordan section).
Neh. 11:25   Resettled following the captivity

» Identified as todays city of Dimona in the northeast Negev about 34 km southeast of Beersheva.

TAMAR

Ezk 47:19   The southern boundary of the land
Ezk 48:28   The southern boundary of Gad

»Tamar is occupied by Mezad Hazeva which is situated on a small hill near the southern bank of Nahal Hazeva in the Arabah. Drive 22.5 km south on route #90 from its junction with #25. The site is just off to west side of the road and is well sign posted. Others locate Tamar further north on route #25, 4 km east of the junction with #258 and 11.4 km west of the junction with #90. The site has remains of a third century Roman fort and lies to the north of the road. The road has recently been rerouted and maps typically show the ruins to the south of the road.

MT. HOR

The most widely accepted location for Mt. Hor is near Petra in Jordan (See Mt. Hor entry in the Jordan section). However, some identify the 278m Har Zin (Har Haran) in the northeastern Negev as Mt. Hor.

Num 20:23-29   Death and burial of Aaron
Num 21:4   Along the route of the exodus
Num 33:38,39   Aaron died at 123 years
Num 34:7,8   Northern boundary of Canaan
Deut 32:50   Aaron died on Mount Hor

» This is tricky because according to most maps Har Zin can only be accessed along a private road, owned by the Negev phosphate plants. However, although this is a private road there are also the ever-present orange Nature Reserve signs. No one could quite explain to us why the Nature Reserve sign posts would direct us along a private road - even the totally obnoxious security guard told us in no uncertain terms to leave the area. So, you have to make your own decision. Although roads come to Mt. Hor from both the west (through Yeroham and Oran), and from the east (from Hazeva) you can only access it from Hazeva. If you come from Yeroham you will arrive at a control barrier as you approach the Oran Phosphate

Plant and the guard will not allow you through (but you could try it); this was the route by which we left the area. From Hazeva, drive 15 km west along route #227. The road then takes a sharp turn to the south and becomes very wide to accommodate the absolutely enormous ore trucks, and very bumpy. Follow the orange Nature Reserve signs for about 6 km and the mountain becomes very obvious when you see it to the south. These directions only bring you to within close viewing distance and do not bring you to the actual mountain. To get to the actual mountain you should contact the Nature Reserves Authority.

ARABAH
'plain, desert'
The name given to the rift valley stretching for 390 km between Mount Hermon in the north, through the Sea of Galilee, the Jordan valley, and the Dead Sea to Eilat. The 'Sea of Arabah' is the Dead Sea.

Deut 1:1	Moses spoke to all Israel
Deut 2:8	Part of the desert wanderings

EILAT
'palm grove'
Two adjacent towns known as Ezion Geber and Elath, located at the head of the Gulf of Aqaba. Ezion Geber is identified with a low mound, Tell el-Kheleifeh, on the Israeli-Jordanian border between Eilat and Aquaba and located about 500m from the present shoreline. This was the twentieth stopping place of the Israelites on their journey from Egypt, and later the naval port of King Solomon. The Queen of Sheba probably passed through Eilat on her way to visit King Solomon.

Num 33:35,36	Children of Israel camped at Ezion Geber
1 Ki 9:26	King Solomon built some of his ships
1 Ki 22:48	Jehoshaphat's fleet wrecked
2 Ki 14:21,22	Azariah rebuilt Elath
2 Chr 8:17-18	Solomon had ships sail for Ophir
2 Chr 20:36-37	Jehoshaphat's fleet wrecked

THE MEDITERRANEAN COAST

*The west border was to the Great Sea
and the coast thereof"
(Jos 15:12)*

GAZA

In Judah (Jos 15:47)
'stronghold'
The most southern and the most famous of the five federated cities of the Philistines.

Jos 11:22	Residence of the 'giant' Anakim
Judg 1:18	Judah captured Gaza and the coast
Judg 16:1-2	Samson slept with a prostitute
Judg 16:3	Samson tore of the gates of the city
Judg 16:21	Samson ground grain as a blinded prisoner
Judg 16:23-30	Samson pushed down the temple pillars
Judg 16:30	Samson's death

» Tel Harube is the site of ancient Gaza situated about 5 km from the sea in the northeastern part of the present city. We never did get to visit Gaza.

ASHKELON

'migration'
This is the birthplace of Herod the Great and one of the five main cities of the Philistines (1 Sam 6:4).

Judg 1:18	Judah captured Ashkelon and the coast
Judg 14:19	Samson killed thirty Philistines ↖
Jer 47:5-7	Jeremiah's oracle against Ashkelon

» It is about 20 km north of Gaza along the coast.

ASHDOD

'fortress'
One of the five main cities of the Philistines. This is New Testament Azotus.

Jos 11:22	Residence of the 'giant' Anakim
1 Sam 5:1-7	Ark of God brought to Dagon's temple
2 Chr 26:5,6	King Uzziah broke down the walls of Ashdod
Is 20:1	Tartan of Assyria captured the city
Amos 1:8	Destruction of Ashdod foretold
Acts 8:40	Philip preached the gospel

» Situated 14 km north of Ashkelon on route #42. Drive south of Ashdod on route #42. For most of the way the road follows alongside the railway. After about 2 km the highway takes a curve away from the railway and after a further 1.5 km comes back to the railway. Just before rejoining the railway the Tel is to the west of the road between the highway and the railway.

Just north of the residential area of modern Ashdod, south of the port and overlooking it, there is a park on top of a hill called Givat Yonah, or the Hill of Jonah. Both Jewish and Moslem traditions hold that Jonah was cast ashore on the beach below this park and from this hill he began his journey to Nineveh (Jonah 3:1-4).

Jonah 1:17-2:10 The great fish vomited Jonah upon the dry
                 land

YAVNEH (JABNEH)
Jabneh is identified with modern Yabneh.
2 Chr 26:6   Uzziah breached the city walls   `
»Jabneh is about 7 km from the coast and 15 km northeast of Ashdod on route #42. The mound is on the southern outskirts of town behind a large MUL-T-LOCK outlet.

JOPPA
'beautiful'
Also Jaffa and Yafo. This was the gateway of ancient Palestine and is now at the southern outskirts of Tel Aviv. It claims to be the oldest port in the world having been commissioned by Japheth the son of Noah.
2 Chr 2:16   Arrival of construction material for temple
Ezra 3:7   Cedar logs brought by sea from Lebanon
Jonah 1:3   Jonah boarded a boat for Tarshish
Acts 9:36-53   Peter raised Tabitha (Dorcas) to life
Acts 10:32   Home of Simon the tanner
Acts 10:9-16   Peter's vision of the sheets from heaven
» The archeological mound of ancient Jaffa is located in Old Jaffa.

LYDDA

LYDDA

Today, and in Old Testament times, it is the town of Lod. Lydda is near Joppa (Acts 9:38).

Acts 9:32-35   Peter healed Aeneas the paralytic

» About 17 km from Tel Aviv and right by Ben Gurion International airport (formerly Lod airport).

VALLEY OF SHARON

The plain along the Mediterranean coast north of Tel Aviv and known for its fertile land (1 Chr 27:29; Is 35:2). Sharon is also called Lasharon (Jos 12:18).

Song 2:1   The Rose of Sharon
Is 33:9   The valley will become like a desert
Acts 9:32-35   The news of Aeneas' healing is heard

ANTIPATRIS - APHEK

'belonging to Antipater'
Antipatris was built on the Plain of Sharon by Herod the Great and named after his father Antipater. It was built on the ruins of ancient Aphek. The large mound is occupied by the remains of a large Turkish citadel built on the remains of a Crusader castle.

Jos 12:1, 18   Joshua defeated the king of Aphek
1 Sam 4:1   Philistines camped before fighting Israelites
1 Sam 4:1-11   The ark of God captured
1 Sam 4:11   Eli's two sons, Hophni and Phinehas, died
1 Sam 29:1   Philistines gathered their forces
1 Ki 20:26   Ben-Hadad gathered the Arameans to fight
1 Ki 20:30   27,000 men killed when a wall collapsed
1 Ki 20:20   Ben-Hadad hid in an inner room
Acts 23:31   Paul passed through on his way to
                 Caesarea

» Tel Rosh ha'Ayin (Arabic Tell Ras el'Aln). It is about 16 km east of Tel Aviv city center and 4 km east of Petah Tikva, near the junction of routes #481 and #444.

EBENEZER

'stone of help'
Many scholars believe that the village of Izbet Sartah is Biblical
Ebenezer.

1 Sam 4	Israelites camped before fighting Philistines
1 Sam 5:1	Ark of God captured
2 Sam 23:14	Philistines had a garrison here

*» The ruins of Ebenezer are in an open area in the community of Rosh
Ha'Ayin. Drive north from Aphek for about 2 km along route #444
to the Qasim junction. Turn east on the Trans-Samaria Hwy (route
#5) in the direction of the West Bank town of Ariel. After 2.5 km veer
to the right following signs to Rosh Ha'Ayin. After only 0.5 km you
can pull off to the right side of the road just before a small stand of
trees. This is the first hill to the south of the road. Climb over the
fence and follow the track for about 250m to the ruins at the top of
the hill. Alternatively, if you don't want to park here you can
continue for an additional 0.8 km and turn right on Nahal Raba St.,
and drive through the settlement to the parking lot at the edge of the
mound. From the parking lot, you have to guess your way in a
general northeastern direction to the ruins at the opposite side of the
mound (about 200m) - careful, there is a steep ledge into a small
quarry in the middle of all this.*

CAESAREA

'pertaining to Caesar'
The Roman capital of Judaea in the time of Christ and Paul.
Herod the Great began to build the city in 25 BC and named it
in honor of Caesar Augustus.

Acts 8:40	Philip preached
Acts 9:29,30	Paul brought here when Grecian Jews tried to kill him
Acts 10:1,24	Cornelius, centurion in the Roman Guard
Acts 10:23b-48	Peter at Cornelius' house
Acts 12:19-23	Herod Agrippa "eaten by worms and died"
Acts 18:22	On Paul's second missionary journey
Acts 21:8	On Paul's third missionary journey

Acts 21:8   Paul stayed at home of Philip the evangelist
Acts 24:1-23   Paul's trial before Felix
Acts 24:27,25:4   Paul in prison
Acts 25:6-12   Paul's trial before Festus
Acts 25:23-26:32 Paul before Agrippa
Acts 27:1-2   Paul sailed, under guard, for Rome

» Located on the Mediterranean coast, 50 km north of Tel Aviv on route #32 and between Tel Aviv and Haifa.

DOR

Allotted to Manasseh, although situated in the territory of Asher (Jos 17:11)

'habitation'

A Canaanite town in the district of Naphoth Dor (Jos 11:2), or, the 'heights of Dor'.

Jos11:2   A town and district of Canaan
Jos12:23   Conquered by Joshua
Judg 1:27   Manasseh failed to drive out the inhabitants
                 of the city
1 Kin 4:11   One of Solomon's tax districts

» Identified with Khirbet el-Burj located on the Mediterranean coast south of Mount Carmel and about 13 km north of Caesarea on route #2. Leave the motorway following the sign to Zikhron Yaaqov. After about 2 km, at a major intersection, turn north following signs to Dor. As you approach Dor the road passes under the motorway, then over the railway. You can either drive straight on to the Nasholim Beach Resort, park, and walk (5 minutes) across the northern end of the beach, or, turn right and park in the kibbutz parking lot close to the ruins. The ruins are one of the largest ecclesiastical complexes excavated in the middle east outside of Jerusalem - and the beach is a beauty.

PLAINS OF ARMAGEDDON AND JEZREEL

CARMEL
'fruit garden, orchard' or 'vineyard of God'

"How long halt ye between two opinion? if the LORD be God,
follow him" (1 Ki 18:20)

A mountain ridge (highest point is 531m) running for about 20
km east southeast from Haifa. In Hebrew, Carmel is Kerem El.

1 Ki 18:19-40 Elijah challenged the prophets of Baal
2 Ki 4:18-25 Shunammite woman sought Elisha

» The traditional location where Elijah challenged the prophets of
Baal is at Muhraka (means 'scorching' or 'the sacrifice') about 28
km south east of Haifa on route #672. The actual site of Elijah's
challenge is of course open to question, but from this site one can see
the Mediterranean Sea (1 Ki 18:43) and the Kishon River (1 Ki
18:45,6). According to some sources there is also a small spring (1
Ki 18:33) just below Carmelite monastery but we have never been
able to locate it.

KISHON RIVER
'curving'
A small stream just north of Mt. Camel which runs from Mt.
Gilboa, along the plain of Megiddo to the sea near Haifa.

Judg 4:7-13 Deborah and Barak pursued Sisera
1 Ki 18:40 Prophets of Baal slaughtered

» Best is to drive route #722 from route #70 across to #75, and cross
the river.

MEGIDDO
In Issachar and Asher but belonged to Manasseh (Jos 17:11)
'place of troops'
The 'chariot city' which guarded the Pass of Megiddo and
overlooking the Jezreel Valley. This is an important site which
has 20 layers of ruined cities. Many important battles were
fought here in Old Testament times and the last great
prophetic battle, the battle of Armageddon is still to be fought

(Zec 12:11). Armageddon is a corruption of Har Megedon, meaning 'mountain of Megiddo.'

Judg 5	Song of Deborah
1 Ki 4:12	The center of a Royal province
1 Ki 9:15	Constructions of Solomon
2 Ki 9:27	Ahaziah king of Judah died here
2 Chr 9:25	One of Solomon's chariot cities

» It is near the junction of routes #65 and #66, 35 km southeast of Haifa

ARMAGEDDON - PLAIN OF MEGIDDO

A part of the wide flat plain running across Israel from Haifa on the coast to Beth Shean in the Jordan Valley. It turns into the Valley of Jezreel to the east. The Greek form of Jezreel is Esdraelon.

Judg 1:27	Manasseh did not drive out these people
2 Ki 23:29	Josiah killed by Pharaoh Neco from Egypt
2 Chr 35:22-24	Josiah killed by Pharaoh Neco from Egypt
Rev 16:12-16	Battle of Armageddon

JEZREEL

In Issachar but belonged to Manasseh (Jos 19:18)
'God scatters'

(Map 20). In Old Testament times this was the name given to the valley separating Samaria from Galilee; the western end of this valley is sometimes called Esdraelon which is Greek for Jezreel. Either King Omri or King Ahab and his wife Jezebel built Jezreel as a second capital of the northern kingdom of Israel.

Judg 1:27-28	Installation of tribes
1 Ki 21:1	A palace of Ahab
1 Ki 21:1-24	Naboth's vineyard
2 Ki 9:33	Jezebel killed by Jehu's followers
2 Ki 10:7-11	Jehu slaughtered seventy sons of Ahab
2 Ki 9:15,16	Ahaziah came to visit king Joram

» The city, between Megiddo and Beth Shean, is perched on the spur of a prominent hill, Mt. Gilboa, overlooking route #71. The ruins are 1.2 km east from the Jezreel (Yizreel) junction with route #60, on route #675, and 2.2 km from the junction with route #71.

TAANACH

In Manasseh (Jos 17:11-13) and reallocated to the Kohathites (Jos 21:25)

Jos 12:21	The king of Taanach defeated by Joshua
Judg 1:27	Manasseh did not drive out the inhabitants of the city
Judg 5:19	Kings of Canaan defeated by Deborah and Barak
1 Ki 4:12	Baana son of Ahilud, one of Solomon's officials, presided here

» The ruins of Taanach, Tel Ta'anach, are on the southwestern edge of the Valley of Jezreel. From Megiddo junction, drive southeast on route #60 towards Jenin for 4 km to an army check point. Soon after the checkpoint you will see the impressive mound to your right. Proceed for a further 2.4 km until you see a signpost to Yabad to the south. Follow this road (#596) for 0.7 km, park in the small village, and follow the track to the mound to your right.

OPHRAH

In Manasseh (Judg 6:24)
(Map 22)

Judg 6:11	Home town of Gideon
Judg 6:24	Gideon built an altar
Judg 6:36-30	Gideon's fleece
Judg 8:22-27	Gideon's ephod
Judg 8:32	Burial place of Gideon
Judg 9:1-5	Abimelech killed seventy of his brothers

» This location is not known with certainty but it may be today's city of Afula. The Tel at Afula is situated within the modern town a few hundred meters from city center. Only a very small part of it has been preserved, most having been destroyed by development. From city center follow map 22.

SHUNEM

In Issachar (Jos 19:18)
(Map 20)

1 Sam 28:4	Philistines camped before battle of Gilboa
1 Ki 1:3	Home of Abishag
2 Ki 4:8-37	Elisha and the Shunammite's son.
Song 6:13	The young woman in the song

» Now the Arab village of Solem about 15 km south of Nazareth in the Valley of Jezreel, and on the lower slopes of Mt. Moreh about 2 km east of Afula off route #71.

MOUNT MOREH

In Issachar
(Map 20). The site has been identified as present-day Jebel Dahi, to the north and bordering the Jezreel Valley. Shunem and Nain are on its lower slopes. The name Moreh is also used for the Oak of Moreh near Shechem.

Judg 7:1	Midianites camped nearby for battle against Gideon

MOUNT GILBOA

perhaps 'bubbling fountain'
A ridge of mountains rising to 475m on the south of the Jezreel Valley across from Mt. Moreh, at the eastern end of the Jezreel valley.

1 Sam 28:4	Saul camped before battle with Philistines
1 Sam 31:1-8	Death of Saul and three sons, including Jonathan

» Follow route #669 for about 6 km west of Beth Shean. A road to the south leads to the summit of Mt. Gilboa.

GIDEONA

Judg 7:1-8   Gideon chose 300 men to fight Midianites

» At the base of Mt. Gilboa, and currently inside a park and picnic area beside Ein Harod Youth Hostel, 10 km east of Afula on route #71.

BETH SHEAN

In Issachar and Asher but belonged to Manasseh (Jos 17:11)
'place of security'
Also Beth Shan (1 Ki 4:12). Situated where the Jezreel Valley slopes down to the west bank of the River Jordan. In New Testament times it was known as Scythopolis, and was the only city of the Decapolis west of the Jordan River. The Tel is 75m high, contains 18 layers of cities, and is one of the largest in Israel. The temple of Dagon, the chief god of the Philistines, has been excavated on the northern slope of the Tel.

Jos 17:16   Joshua's troops could not deal with iron
                 chariots
Judg 1:27   Manasseh did not drive out these people
1 Sam 31:8-12   Saul and Jonathan's body fastened to the
                 city wall
2 Sam 21:12   Citizens of Jabesh Gilead removed bones
                 of Saul and Jonathan
1 Chr 10:10   Saul's head fastened in the temple of Dagon.

ABEL MEHOLA

In Issachar
'meadow of dancing'
Judg 7:22   Gideon pursued the Midianites
1 Sam 18:19   Adriel married Saul's daughter Merab
1 Ki 4:12   Baana was Solomon's governor
1 Ki 19:16   Home of Elisha son of Shaphat
1 Ki 19:19-21   Elijah called Elisha to the ministry

» Of uncertain location but the name is carried on by the village of Mehola about 20 km south of Beth Shean on route #90 in the Jordan valley. Maybe Tel Maqlub east of the Jordan River by Wadi Yabis in

the hill country of Gilead, or, Tel Abu Sus about 5 km northeast of today's collective farming village of Mehola. From Mehola drive south about 1 km until the road takes a fairly sharp right turn and goes down a short hill to the valley bottom. As you start going down hill a poorly paved road takes off to the left. Follow this for 0.6 km to a sharp left, then for another 1.3 km to a junction. Turn right and drive as far as you are able, probably no more than 0.6 km and Tel Abu Sus is straight ahead of you and very close to the Israeli-Jordanian border.

GALILEE

ACCO
In Asher (Judg 1:31)
'hot sand'
This is New Testament Ptolemais.
Acts 21:7   Paul landed here by boat from Tyre

SHIMRON-MERON
'guard'
A royal city of the Canaanites. This is Tel es-Semuniyeh or Tel Shimron.
Jos 11:1   Joined forces with Jabin against Joshua
» This is a rather uninteresting Tel about 5 km west of Nazareth on route #75. It is on the northeast corner of the junction that leads north to the village of Zarzir.

NAZARETH
In Zebulun
'watchtower'
(Map 20)
Mt 2:23   Jesus lived in Nazareth
Mt 13:53-58   A prophet is without respect in his own house
Lk 1:26-38   Angel Gabriel appeared to Mary; the annunciation
Lk 2:39,51   Jesus' boyhood in Nazareth
Lk 4:15-30   Jesus in the synagogue; attempt to kill Him

SEPPHORIS
(Map 20). The traditional home of Joachim and Anne, Mary's parents, and the birthplace of the virgin Mary. The Latin name for the ancient city and modern settlement is Tzipori. This was the capital of Galilee in Herod's time. As a child, Jesus lived only 5 km from here and probably visited this major city of over 30000 inhabitants on many occasions. Tzipori was a wealthy city, the seat of the Jewish Sanhedrin for several years, and here the Mishna (codification of the oral law)was compiled around 200AD. Josephus called Sepphoris "the ornament of

Galilee." Finds at Sepphoris include a Roman villa, a large Roman reservoir and aqueduct, a Roman theatre, a market building with mosaics, and a large mosaic floor with mythological scenes including the extraordinary "Mona Lisa of the Galilee."

» The impressive ruins of ancient Tzipori are about 5 km northwest of Nazareth, just off route #79.

CANA

'place of reeds'
(Maps 20&24)

Jn 2:1-11	Wedding, and the water turned into wine
Jn 4:46-54	Cure of government official's son
Jn 21:2	Nathanael was from Cana

»Identified with Kefr Kenna 11 km northeast of Nazareth on route #754 to Capernaum. However, apologies to all of you travelers who have visited the wrong site for years! The probable location of the original, real, 'Cana of Galilee' is about 5 km further north to the southwest of Har near Mt. Atzmon. This one requires effort. Enter the village of Kafr Manda until you reach a turning circle which has seven different streets merging. Follow map 24. You will drive a fairly rough dirt track east beyond Kafr Manda for 4.2 km.

GATH HEPHER

(Map 20). Also called Gittahhepher (Jos 19:13). Arab tradition places Jonah's tomb in the base of the village Muslim mosque. However, Jonah is also purportedly buried in the village of Halhul about 7 km north of Hebron just to the east of route #60.

2 Ki 14:25	Birthplace of the prophet Jonah

» Now the Arab village of Mashhad, about 10 km north of Nazareth and 2 km before Cana

---

NAIN
'delightful'
(Maps 20 & 23)
Lk 7:11-17   Widow's son brought back to life
» Today's village of Nein on the northern slope of Mt. Moreh and about 6 km northeast of Afula on route #65. The disused village church has a mural describing the story of Christ restoring life to the widow's son. The church is locked but the family beside the church has a key. Follow Map 23 to the church.

ENDOR
In Issachar and Asher but belonged to Manasseh (Jos 17:11)
'fountain of habitation'
(Maps 20 & 23)
1 Sam 28:7-25   Saul visited the witch of Endor
» The name is maintained today by Kibbutz Ein Dor 4 km east of Mt. Tabor. The original location is assumed to be Tel Zafzafot (Tel el-Ajul) about 4 km southwest of the kibbutz and 8 km northeast of Afula on route #65. Exact location not certain but turn off route #65 to the east following the sign to Tamra. After 1.1 km the road forks. The original site was probably on the mound between the two roads. The word 'en' or 'ein' means spring, and the location of the spring may be a little more definite. Take the left fork and drive for 1.4 km. At this point a very well travelled track leaves the road to the left and winds through the fields for about 1 km. You can follow the map but you can quite easily see your destination which has nine fairly large palm trees.

MOUNT TABOR
'height'
(Map 20). A 500m steep-sided mountain rising from the Plain of Jezreel. It is situated where the borders of Issachar, Zebulun and Napthali meet. One of the traditional sites of the Transfiguration although other authorities place this event at Mt. Hermon in northeastern Israel.
Judg 4:5-16   Victory of Barak and Deborah over Sisera

Judg 8:18,19   Midianite kings killed the brothers of Gideon
Hos 5:1   A place of worship since ancient times
Mt 17:1-9   Transfiguration of Christ
    Also: Mk 9:2-8; Lk 9:28-36
» Mt. Tabor is 14 km northeast of Afula on route #65.

DABARAH

In Issachar (Jos 19:12; 21:18), and assigned as a Levitical city (1 Chr 6:72).
'a pasture'
(Map 20). Also spelled Daberath (NIV).
» The village of Deburiyeh is on the western slope of Mt. Tabor on the road that encircles the mount.

ZAANANNIM

In Naphtali (Jos 19:33)
(Map 20). Also spelled Zaanaim (Judg 4:11). This location is generally accepted to be the site of today's Khan et-Tuggar (Hanot Tagarim).
Jos 19:33   A large terebinth tree nearby
Judg 4:11   Heber the Kenite camped here
» Travel northeast on route #65 until Tavor Junction. Travel beyond the junction on route #65 for almost 4 km until you see a sign to Bet Qeshet to the left. Some of the ruins, mostly Ottoman and Mamluk, are to the right at the junction.

"From the plain to the Sea of Chinneroth
(Jos 12:3).

AREA AROUND THE SEA OF GALILEE

(Map 25). The Sea of Galilee is a fresh-water lake. It is also known as the Lake of Gennesaret (Lk 5:1), and the Sea of Tiberias (Jn 6:1; 21:1). In the Old Testament it was known as the Sea of Chinnereth (Num 34:11; Deut 3:17; Jos 11:2; 13:27). It is more than 230m below sea level, ranges from 25-50m deep, is 22 km long and 12 km wide. Many Bible

events are recorded but all we know is that they happened on or around the Sea of Galilee and no exact location is given. Of Jesus' 33 major miracles, 25 occurred around the Sea of Galilee. Many events are written in more than one of the gospels and these references will not normally be duplicated.

Mt 4:18-22;9:9	Call of the first apostles Also: Mk 1:16-20;2:14; Lk 5:2-11,27; Jn 1:35-43
Lk 5:12-14	Cure of the leper
Mt 8:23-27	Calming the storm Also: Mk 4:36-41; Lk 8:22-25
Mt 9:18-24	Resurrection of Jairus' daughter Also: Mk 5:22-43; Lk 8:40-56
Mt 9:20-22	Jesus healed the sick woman Also: Mk 5:25-34; Lk 8:43-48
Mt 12:1-8	Picking corn on the Sabbath Also: Mk 2:23-28; Lk 6:1-5
Mt 12:9-14	Cure of man with paralyzed hand Also: Mk 3:1-6; Lk 6:6-11
Mt 14:22-33	Walking on the water Also: Mk 6:45-51; Jn 6:16-21

TIBERIAS

(Map 25). One of the four Jewish holy cities (along with Hebron, Jerusalem and Tiberias).

Jn 6:23   People got boats to follow Jesus.

» Tiberias is the major town on the western shore of the Sea of Galilee.

MIGDAL; MAGDALA

(Map 25). Also called Magadan (Mt 15:39) and Dalmanutha (Mk 8:10).

Lk 8:1-2   Town of Mary Magdalene

» On the western shore of the Sea of Galilee about 6 km north of Tiberias on route #90.

TABGHA

(Map 25). The Arabic name Tabgha comes from the earlier Greek Heptapegon meaning seven springs. There are two different sites here about 300m apart. This is the traditional location where Jesus baptized the apostles. It is also the traditional site of Jesus' miracle of the feeding of the multitude even though the gospels firmly place the miracle at Bethsaida (Lk 9:10-17).

Church of the Multiplication of the Loaves and Fishes

Mt 14:13-21	Miracle of the feeding of the 5000 men
	Also: Mk 6:30-44; Jn 6:1-14

Church of St. Peter

Jn 21:4-11	The miraculous catch of fish
Jn 21:12-14	Jesus' third post resurrection appearance
Jn 21:15-19	Jesus reinstated Peter

» Situated on route #87 about 1 km east of the junction with route #90

MOUNT OF BEATITUDES

(Map 25). Traditional site from which Jesus delivered the sermon on the mount (Mt cpts. 5, 6 and 7). The octagonal church on the site was built to commemorate the eight beatitudes. Among the more famous passages of the sermon are:

Mt 5:3-11	"Blessed are the poor in spirit .."
Mt 5:13-16	"You are the salt .. the light .."
Mt 6:9-13	"Our Father which art in heaven .."
Mt 6:19-23	"Lay up for yourselves treasure in heaven
Mt 6:24	"No man can serve two masters .."
Mt 6:33	"But seek ye first the kingdom of God .."
Mt 5:1-12	The beatitudes
Mt 6:5-15	Jesus taught about prayer
Mt 7:7-12	Ask, seek, and knock
Mt 7:13-14	Narrow and wide gates
Mt 7:24-27	The wise and foolish builders

» Some sects propose that the sermon may have been delivered on the Horns of Hittim, some 10 km west of Tiberias on route #77 to Nazareth, and site of a famous Crusader defeat by the Moslem army of Saladin in 1187.

KORAZIM
'secret'
(Map 25)

Mt 11:21	Jesus performed miracles
Mt 11:20-22	Curse on Korazim, Bethsaida, and Capernaum. Also: Lk 10:13-15

» Now identified with ruins about 4 km north of Capernaum. Travel north along route #90 for about 3 km north of the Mt. of Beatitudes. Turn east and follow the signs for 2 km to the ruins.

CAPERNAUM
'village of Nahum' - perhaps Nahum the prophet but we can't be certain.

(Map 25). Capernaum was the chief social and commercial center of this area during the ministry of Jesus. It was Jesus' base while He was teaching in Galilee, and is sometimes referred to as "his own city" (Mt 9:1; Mk 2:1). This may have been the home town of the prophet Nahum.

Mt 8:5-13	The centurion's son healed Also: Lk 7:1-10; Jn 4:46-50
Mt 9:1	Capernaum became Jesus' town
Mt 9:2-8	Man let down through the roof (Peter's house) Also: Mk 2:3-12; Lk 5:18-26
Mt 9:9-12	Calling of Matthew Also: Mk 2:14-17; Lk 5:27-32
Mt 11:21	Jesus performed miracles
Mt 11:20-22;	Curse on Korazim, Bethsaida, and Capernaum. Also: Lk 10:13-15
Mt 8:14,15	Cure of Peter's mother-in-law Also: Mk 1:29-31; Lk 4:38,39
Mk 1:21	Jesus taught in the synagogue

Also: Lk 4:31-38; Jn 6:59
Mk 1:29   Peter and Andrew lived here for time
» Located on the northwest shore of the Sea of Galilee on route #87
about 5 km east of the junction with route #90.

BETHSAIDA
'house of fishing'
(Map 25) This is Old testament Ziddim (Jos 19:35).
Mt 11:21   Jesus performed miracles
Mt 11:20-22   Curse on Korazim, Bethsaida, and
                 Capernaum. Also: Lk 10:13-15
Mk 8:22-26   Healing of a blind man
Lk 9:10-17   Jesus fed the multitude
                 Also: Mt 14:13-21; Mk 6:30-44; Jn 6:1-14
Jn 1:44   Home town of Philip, Andrew and Peter
*» There may have been two different Bethsaidas. One has been
identified as Et-Tell in Hayarden (The Jordan) Park, about 3 km
north of where the River Jordan enters the Sea of Galilee. Drive 2
km east of the rumble bridge over the River Jordan, and turn left on
route #888 for 1.3 km. Turn left into the park and follow directions
to the excavations. This is a particularly interesting site because
excavators have unearthed a piece of Roman pavement which means
you can literally walk where Jesus walked.*

TEL HADAR
'splendid hill'
*(Map 25). We know the geographic location of Geshur from
various passages (Num 21:33-35; Deut 3:1-14; 2 Sam 15:8).
Today the area is known as the southern Golan. At least five
sites in the area have been excavated. The excavations at Tel
Hadar indicate that this was a major Geshurite stronghold and
perhaps the one to which Absalom fled.*
2 Sam 3:3   Absalom's mother was a Geshurite princess
2 Sam 13:37-39 Absalom fled here after murdering Amnon
Mt 15:29-39   Miracle of the feeding of the 4000 men
                 Also: Mk 8:1-10

Arise, walk through the land

» The Tel is 2.2 km north of Kursi on route #92 along the eastern shore of the Sea of Galilee; follow the signs to Golan Beach. About 100m after passing through the park gate you will find the Tel on your left.

GADARA
'walls'

(Map 25). Scholars have not yet positively identified 'Gadarenes' (Lk 8:26) or 'Gergesenes' (Mt 8:28). Gadarenes refers to the city of Gadara (refer to entry in the Jordan section) which was one of the cities of the Decapolis and its territory extended to include the famous hot springs at today's Roman ruins at Hamat Gadar. Likewise, Gergesenes refers to the city of Gerasa (modern Jaresh - see entry in Jordan section). It is not likely that either of these two origins is correct. Since the 4th century, tradition has identified Gergesa with the site of Kursi on the eastern shore of the Sea of Galilee opposite Tiberias. Recently there has been a suggestion that Kursi was the site of the feeding of the 4000 and that the swine-miracle took place about 12 km further to the south near Tel Samra. However, confusion of the names makes identification difficult.

Mt 8:28-32   Gergesenes; pigs ran into the sea
Mk 5:1-20   Cure of the demoniac at Gadara
Lk 8:26-33   Gadarenes; pigs ran into the sea

» The ruins of Gadara are at present-day Umm Qeis about 10 km southeast of the Sea of Galilee, in Jordan. Kursi is at the intersection of routes #92 and #789. Hamat Gadar hot springs are just off route #98 about 7 km southeast of the Sea of Galilee on the river Yarmuk.

HIPPOS

(Map 25). This is Tel Sussita and was one of the cities of the Decapolis on the eastern shore of the Sea of Galilee. The Greeks called it Hippos meaning 'a horse' and Jews called the city Sussita which is Aramaic for 'mare'. Later Arab conquerors named it Qal'at el Husn, or 'fortress of the horse'. It may be the Aphek of 1 and 2 Kings, the name being preserved by the nearby village of Afiq. Hippos is not

*specifically mentioned as a Biblical site but it was probably
visited by Jesus during His ministry in Galilee. This may have
been the city set on a hill in Mt 5:14 although this traditionally
is given as Safed.*

1 Ki 20:26, 30   Ben-Hadad fought Israel

2 Ki 13:17   Arameans defeat predicted

*» The ruins are high on the hill above kibbutz En Gev. Take the road
to the east which branches of route #92 about 1 km south of En Gev.
Drive 3.3 km, almost to the top of the hill, until you come to the very
obvious path to the ruins.*

PILGRIMS' BAPTISMAL SITE

2 Ki 5:1-14   Naaman perhaps (?) healed of his leprosy
                     close by

*» A designated site on the River Jordan a few hundred meters
downstream from where the river exits the Sea of Galilee near
Deganya.*

JOSEPH'S WELL

*(Map 25). Dothan in northern Samaria is the location (Gen
37:12,17) where Joseph's brothers put him into a well (see
Dothan entry). However, Arab tradition places the well on
Kibbutz Ammi'ad. The accommodation on the kibbutz is called
"Joseph's Well Country Inn" Arab tradition also places the
tomb of Joshua much further north than generally accepted
(see entry for Joshua's tomb).*

Gen 37:12-28   Joseph placed in a pit, or cistern

*» Travel north on route #90 for about 4 km beyond the Mt. of
Beatitudes to Ammi'ad junction. Carry on beyond the junction with
route #85 (Ammi'ad junction.) for a short distance and the kibbutz in
on the left. The well is easy to get to but you will never find it without
directions from the people on the kibbutz. Like Joshua's tomb further
north, it is also a domed structure - and it's not very deep!*

SAFED

One of the four Jewish holy cities (along with Hebron, Jerusalem and Tiberias) and the center of Jewish mysticism, this city can be clearly seen from the Sea of Galilee and from great distances around.

Mt 5:14   A city set on a hill cannot be hid

» Safed is 10 km west of Rosh Pina on route #89.

HAZOR

'an enclosure' or 'settlement'.

Hazor is the largest and most important archeological mound in northern Israel, and was once an important royal city. There are four other sites with this same name. Two sites of unknown location in southern Judah (Jos 15:23,25), one in Benjamin (Neh 11:33), and an unidentified one which was attacked by Nebuchadnezzar (Jer 49:28-33).

Judg 1-24   Sisera, commander of Hazor's armies

Jos 11:1-14   Joshua destroyed the city and killed its king defeated

Judg 4:1,2   Jabin, a king of Canaan, reigned here

1 Ki 9:15   One of Solomon's "chariot cities"

2 Ki 15:29   People taken captive by Assyrians

»Now called Tel el-Qedah, and is 8 km north of Rosh Pina on route #90.

MEROM

'high place'

Now maintained as the Huleh Nature Reserve.

Jos 11:5-7   Joshua defeated Jabin, king of Hazor

» Probably the lake of the Huleh on the River Jordan, about 25 km north of the Sea of Galilee on route #90.

JOSHUA'S TOMB

There are at least two other traditional locations for the burial place of Joshua, both of them in Samaria (see Timnath Serah entry). This particular location is mainly revered by a Shi'ite

Muslim sect.

» Travel north on route #90 to the Koah junction 10 km north of Hazor. Turn left on route #899 and climb the scenic road for 4 km to Yesha junction. Park and look over the fence in the southeastern corner of the junction. The double-domed structure is easily seen.

KEDESH

In Naphtali (Jos 19:37; Judg 4:6), and allotted to the Levites.
'holy'
In the King James it is called Kedesh-naphtali. This is Tel Kades. There are a few scattered stones, It is a bit overgrown, and generally not much to see here. There are two other Old Testament towns with this name, one in southern Judah (Jos 15:23) and one in Issachar (1 Chr 6:72) also called Kishion (Jos 19:20) and Kishon (Jos 21:28). There may also be another Kedesh, also in Naphtali, which was captured by Joshua (Jos 12:22), was the home of Barak (Judg 4:6), and the city in which Deborah and Barak gathered their forces to fight Sisera. However, scholars are in disagreement as to whether these are in fact two different cities, or one and the same.

Jos 20:7; 21:32   A city of refuge
2 Ki 15:29   Conquered by king of Assyria

» Continue along route #899 for 2.4 km beyond Yesha junction. You will come to a parking spot at the entrance to a private road to the right. Park in this spot and walk on to the tel.

ABEL-BETH MAACAH

In Napthali
'meadow of the house of oppression'
Also called Abel (2 Sam 20:18) and Abel Maim (2 Chr 16:4).
2 Sam 20:13-21   Joab hunted down the rebel Sheba
2 Sam 20:21-22   Sheba's head thrown from the city wall
1 Ki 15:20   Captured by Ben-Hadad of Syria
2 Ki 15:29   Captured by Tiglath-Pileser of Assyria

» Now identified as Tel Abil el-Qamh (heb. Tel Avel Bet Ma'akha) about 2 km south of Metulla on route #90 and about 10 km west of Dan.

DAN
'a judge'
Called Laish before it was captured by the Danites (Judg 18:29) and called Leshem in Jos 19:47. Throughout the settled history of Israel, Dan was recognized as the northern border of the country. The largest spring in the Bible lands, if not in the world, arises from the western end of the mound, and is the largest and most important of the three sources of the River Jordan (Dan River). On the mound are a number of interesting archeological finds including a 'high place' which may have been that built by King Jeroboam (1 Ki 12:26-31) when he caused Israel to sin. At the eastern edge of the Tel is the only mud-brick gate in the Near East to have survived intact and it dates back to about 1800BC - yes, perhaps Abraham passed through this gate!

Judg 18:1-31	Danites settled in Laish
2 Sam 3:10	From Dan to Beersheva (see Beersheva)
	Also: 2 Sam 17:11;2 Sam 24:2;1 Ki 4:25;
	2 Chr 30:5
1 Ki 12:26-31	King Jeroboam made a golden calf and
	built an altar

» Tel Dan (arab. Tel el-Qadi), is 11 km east of Qiryat Shemona on route #99.

CAESAREA PHILIPPI
'Caesar's city of Philippi'
Biblical Caesarea Philippi is located at Banias Springs, at the southern base of Mt. Hermon. These springs are one of the major sources of the River Jordan. The name Banias is a corruption of Paneas, a sacred place to the god Pan. At the site one can still see a few reminders of this pagan worship.

Mt 16:13-20	Peter's confession of Christ
	Also: Mk 8:27-30; Lk 9:18-21

» Banias Springs are 4.3 km east of Dan. Extensive new digging is occurring about 100m down the road from the entrance to the springs, on the opposite side of the road. Some ruins of ancient Caesarea Philippi are visible to the north of the road about 300m before Banias on the road from Dan.

MOUNT HERMON
'sacred mountain'
In the extreme north of Israel and over 2750m high. It's proximity to Caesarea Philippi and its height make a more likely site of the transfiguration than Mt.Tabor.
Deut 3:8-9   The land taken as far as Mt. Hermon
» Drive route #98 to the village of Majdal Shams and ask some of the very friendly local Druze to show you the "shouting valley". Continue driving for about 20 minutes until you come to the ski area. The cable car will bring you to almost the highest point in the Israeli part of the Hermon range. The Syrian Hermon rises another 800m but is in a very strict military area.

BASHAN
Allotted to the half-tribe of Manasseh (Deut. 3:13)
'fertile plain'
The region east of the Jordan River and the Sea of Galilee, and extending from the Yarmouk River in the south to Mt. Hermon in the north; it corresponds approximately to today's Golan Heights. It is a fertile upland area about 500 - 700m above sea level. It was a prosperous and productive region (Is 33:9; Jer 50:19; Mic 7:14) with oak forests (Is 2:13 Ezk 27:5,6 Zech 11:2). Evil people who attacked the righteous were called "strong bulls of Bashan" (Ps. 22:12) and the self-indulgent women of Samaria were called "cows of Bashan" (Amos 4:1). The mountain of Bashan (Ps. 68:15) is probably another name for Mount Hermon.
Num 21:33   Og was the king of Bashan
Deut 3:1-4   Israel defeated the 60 cities of Og
Deut 3:13   Bashan was called the land of giants.

Arise, walk through the land

Deut 29:7	Israel defeated Og the king of Bashan
Deut 32:14	Distinguished for its fine cattle
Jos 13:12	Og reigned in Ashtaroth
Jos 21:27	City of Golan was a city of refuge
2 Ki 10:32,33	Region captured by king Hazael
2 Ki 13:25	Jehoash recaptured the region

EGYPT

*"And Joseph went out .. and traveled
throughout Egypt."
(Gen 41:54,46)*

EGYPT

Gen 12:10	Abram went to live in Egypt
Gen 12:11-20	Abram lied to Pharaoh about Sarah being his sister
Gen 37-Exod 14	From Joseph to the Exodus
Is 19	A prophecy about Egypt
Ezk 30	A lament for Egypt

MEMPHIS

'haven of good'
About 20 km south of Cairo and capital during the Old Kingdom period of Egypt's history (about 3000 BC to 2200 BC). Numerous pyramids, including the world's oldest (Zozer's ca. 2600 BC), are situated nearby.

Is 19:13	The leaders of Memphis are deceived
Jer 44:1	Jeremiah wrote concerning Jews
Jer 46:14-19	Destruction of Memphis foretold
Ezk 30:13,16	God will destroy the images in Memphis

THEBES

Today's city of Luxor. The ancient capital city of upper Egypt on the River Nile about 530 km south of modern Cairo. Thebes was the center of the cult of the god Amun and Jer 46:25; Ezk 30:14 and Neh 3:8 should be seen in this light.

Jer 46:25	Punishment of Thebes foretold
Ezk 30:14-16	God will inflict punishment on Thebes
Nah 3:8	Is Nineveh better than Thebes?

ASWAN

Just as Israel was defined as "from Dan to Beersheva" so Egypt was defined as "from the tower of Syene to the border of Ethiopia" The Egyptian-Ethiopian border was at the first cataract on the Nile, at today's Aswan (NIV says "from Migdol to Aswan").

Ezk 29:10	Egypt will be destroyed from Migdol to Aswan

MOUNT SINAI

Mt. Sinai is called The Mountain of God (Ex 24:13-16, 27) and is also known as Mt. Horeb (Ex 3:1). The search for Mt. Sinai is one of the most intriguing and troublesome problems for archeologists. There are over 20 proposed locations for Mt. Sinai. The most widely accepted one in the southern Sinai has been accepted since the 3rd or 4th cent. AD, but the site's real location has been lost for over 3000 years. Paul said Mt. Sinai was in Arabia. Arabia in the ancient Greek and Roman texts referred to the territories inhabited by Arabs; this includes the Sinai. Quite a different meaning than from today where it refers to Saudi Arabia. The name Mt. Sinai is mentioned 13 times in Exodus but Horeb only twice; Mt. Horeb is used repeatedly in Deuteronomy, but Sinai is absent. This has lead some scholars to argue that these are two separate mountains. However, if we compare Num 33:14, 15 and Ex 19:2,3 it is clear that these names are synonymous.

Gebel Musa, or Mount Moses behind St. Catherine's monastery in the southern Sinai desert is the most widely accepted; it is 2282m high. Gebel Musa has a broad plain near its base, where the children of Israel may have camped. The Sinai desert is described as "a vast and dreadful desert" (Deut 1:19). There is one, not widely accepted theory, that Mt. Sinai is Har Karkom, located in the western Negev about 40 km southwest of Mitzpeh Ramon (see Negev Desert).

Ex 2:15-22	The home of Jethro and his daughters
Ex 3:1-5	Moses and the burning bush
Ex 17:6	Moses struck the rock to get water
Ex 19:18	Mt. Sinai trembled violently
Ex 19:19:20	The Lord descended to the mountain top
Ex 24:16	The glory of the Lord settled on the mount
Ex 20:1-17	Moses and the ten commandments
Ex 21-32	God gave many laws and commandments
Ex 31:18	Stone tablets inscribed by the finger of God
Ex 33:22	Moses put in the cleft of the rock

Arise, walk through the land

Ex 35:29	Moses' face radiant after he had spoken with God
Lev 26:46	Most of the law was given on this mount
1 Ki 19:8	Elijah fled to Mt. Horeb

KADESH, KADESH-BARNEA

It is not easy to get to Kadesh Barnea. It is in the northeastern Sinai desert about half way between the Mediterranean and the Red Seas. I have not been there personally. It seems the only effective way to get there is to hire a taxi from either of the two border crossings between Israel and Egypt - and when you get close, be prepared to walk the last few kilometers. For a fuller coverage of this site, refer to the Kadesh Barnea entry in the Negev section of this book.

JORDAN

KING'S HIGHWAY

This was the main highway in Biblical times running through Edom, Moab and the land of the Ammonites. Today it links the port city of Aqaba in the south with the capital Amman. It passes close to Petra and goes through Karak and Medeba, and crosses the very deep Wadi al-Mujib, hence local people call it the Wadi al-Mujib highway. It is likely that Chedorlaomer and his allied kings approached Sodom and Gomorrah along this route, and that Abraham pursued them back along this way (Gen 14).

Num 20:17	Israel requested passage through Edom
Num 21:22	Passage requested through the Amorites' land

SELA - PETRA

'rock, cliff'
Sela was the capital of Edom. The Nabateans captured Sela and carved the city of Petra (Greek for 'rock') out of the rocky valley at the foot of the original settlement. Petra is located near. Seir in southern Jordan (see Deut 2:4). Some scholars propose that Petra is Biblical Bozrah (means 'sheepfold'; Gen 36:33; 1 Chr 1:44), although Bozrah is usually identified with modern Buseirah, a fortified city about 60 km north of Petra on the King's Highway. Petra, and perhaps Bozrah, is the likely location where the Jewish remnant will flee from Antichrist during the middle of the tribulation. There is also a Sela in Judah (Judg 1:36) and in Moab (Is 16:1).

2 Ki 14:7	Amaziah King of Judah captured Sela in battle
2 Ki 14:7	Amaziah renamed Sela as Joktheel
2 Chr 25:12	Amaziah killed 10000 Edomites from a cliff
Mt 24:15-21	Remnant of Israel will flee to the mountains
Rev 12:6, 14	Israel will flee in the middle of the tribulation

MOUNT HOR

The word Hor is usually regarded as an archaic form of Har, the Hebrew word for "mountain." Mt. Hor is on the border of Edom (Num 20:23). There are at least three contenders for this location. Early tradition established Jebel Harun, meaning "Aaron's Mountain," as the site of Mount Hor. Jebel Harun (1440m) is near Petra on the eastern side of the Arabah. A second is Jebul Madurah close to Kadesh Barnea about 16 km inside the Egyptian border from Israel. A third option is Har Zin or Har Haran near the Oran phosphate plants in the Negev desert (see Mount Hor entry in a previous section "Negev Desert") There is also a Mt. Hor in northern Israel between the Mediterranean Sea and the approach to Hamath (Num 34:7,8) but the exact site of this mountain is unknown.

Num 20:23-29	Death and burial of Aaron
Num 21:4	Along the route of the exodus
Num 33:38,39	Aaron died at 123 years
Num 34:7,8	Northern boundary of Canaan
Deut 32:50	Aaron died on Mount Hor

» There is an easy way and two difficult ways to see Jebul Harun. First the good news. If you drive about 7-10 km south of Petra along the King's Highway you can see a prominent white church planted high on top of the peak away in the distance to the west. The church reportedly houses the tomb of Aaron. Alternatively, you can take the quite arduous but breathtakingly beautiful walk (= climb) to one of Petra's most amazing ruins - the monastery. From the monastery there is a viewpoint across the valley to Jebel Harun. Third, you can hire a guide at the entrance to Petra and climb for about 6 hours to the peak! Regulations require a guide; you can not do this journey alone.

EDOM

The land inhabited by the descendants of Esau (Gen 32:3; 36:8). Many references in the Bible and frequently referred to by the prophets Isaiah, Amos, Obadiah and Malachi. Edom is essentially today's southern Jordan region.

| 2 Ki 3:8 | Kings Joram and Jehoshaphat went to fight Moab |
| 1 Chr 1:43-54 | Rulers and kings of Edom |

CITIES OF THE PLAINS

A term used for the five cities at the southeast end of the Dead Sea - Sodom, Gomorrah, Admah, Zeboiim and Bela (that is Zoar, Gen 14:2,8). Four of these were completely destroyed because of their wickedness (Gen 19:28-30). The exact location of these is uncertain. Some argue that they were located in the flat plain just north of the Dead Sea because Abraham and Lot looked at these cities from somewhere near Bethel (Gen 13:10). Also, there is a prevalent view that they were located beneath the shallow waters of the southern basin of the Dead Sea. However, after extensive excavation in the 1970's, five sites were described in a region to the southeast of the Dead Sea: Bab Edh-Dhra, Numeira, Safi, Feifeh, and Hanzir. All are located by oases. Before their destruction, this area was productive and compared to the garden of Eden and to Egypt (Gen 13:10).

| Gen 13:12 | Lot chose to live in this region, near Sodom |

SODOM AND GOMORRAH

'place of lime'

(Map 26). Bad Edh-Dhra and Numeira may be Sodom and Gomorrah respectively, although some suggest that Sodom may be located further south at either Numeira or Feifeh

Gen 13:10-13	Lot lives in Sodom
Gen 14:11	Two cities plundered
Gen 14:13	Abram's nephew, Lot, is kidnapped
Gen 19:1-29	Sodom and Gomorrah destroyed
Jer 50:40	No one will live in Sodom and Gomorrah

» Bab Edh-Dhra is located about 25 km west of Karak on route #80. Between 5 km and 1.5 km from the junction of route #80 with the Arabah road (route #65) are three mounds. The first has a rather large house on it, the second simply looks like a huge pile of dirt, and the third is fenced; the latter is the site of Bab Edh-Dhra. Numeira is

13.5 km south of the junction along the Arabah road. You will arrive at an elaborate monument to an employee of the Jordanian Potash works on the west side of the road. Almost directly opposite and about 300m to the east of the road on a spur of the hill are the ruins of Numeira. The ascent is quite short, quite steep, and not for the faint-hearted.

ZOAR
'little'
Also called Bela (Gen 14:2,8).

Gen 19:30	After his escape from Sodom, Lot lived in a cave near Zoar
Gen 19:31-38	Lot got drunk and slept with his two daughters

» Zoar is tentatively identified as es-Safi which is about 13 km south of Numeira. It is about 7 km up the River Zered from where it empties into the Dead Sea.

MOAB
"..for whither thou goest, I will go; and where thou lodgest, I will lodge: thy people shall be my people, and thy God my God" (Ruth 1:16)

The land of Moab was settled by the descendants of Lot's son (Gen 19:37). Generally, this is the mid-Jordan region adjacent to the Dead Sea between Edom and Ammon.

Gen 19:36,37	Lot's oldest daughter mother of the Moabites
Num 32:1-37	Reuben and Gad settled in northern Moab
Ruth 1:1-2	Elimelech, Naomi and sons went to live in Moab
Ruth 1:4	Ruth and Orpah were from Moab
2 Ki 3	Moab revolts against King Joram
Job 1:1	Job was from the land of Uz which includes Moab

KIR-HARASETH

The site of this Biblical city is now occupied by the modern city of Karak about halfway along the King's Highway between Petra and Amman.

2 Ki 3:24-27   King of Moab sacrificed his son

RIVER ARNON

In Reuben (Jos 13:16) and Gad (Deut 3:16)

'roaring stream'

This is today's Wadi al-Mujib and is one of the most spectacular sights in Jordan. Known as Jordan's Grand Canyon, the canyon is over 1000m deep and 4 km wide. The Arnon formed a natural boundary between Moabites in the south and the Amorites in the north (Deut 3:16; Num 21:13).

Num 21:13   Camp during the exodus
Num 21:23,26   Israel defeated Sihon
Num 22:36   Balak met Balaam
Deut 2:24   Part of the exodus route

» Drive about 50 km north of Karak on the King's Highway, and guaranteed, you will not miss it. The road winds rather precariously down the southern slope, crosses the wadi, and climbs quite rapidly up an easier northern slope.

AROER

In Reuben and Gad (Deut 3:12)

'ruins'

There are two other towns in the Old Testament with this name; one was a town of Gilead, of unknown location, situated east of Rabbah (Num 32:34). Second was a town in southern Judah (see Aroer entry in Negev Desert section). Aroer was the southernmost town of the northern kingdom of Israel, and it was the southern limit of the Amorite kingdom of Sihon. It was known as "the Beersheva of the East."

Num 32:34   Rebuilt by the Gadites
Deut 2:36   Conquered by Israelites
Deut 4:48   Conquered by Israelites

Judg 11:26   Israel occupied Aroer for 300 years
Judg 11:33   Jephthah devastated the Ammonites
2 Ki 10:33   Taken by Hazael
Is 17:1-3   Isaiah prophesied against Aroer
Jer 48:19   A warning to the people

» Aroer is located at Khirbet Ara'ir, 4 km east of the Karak-Medeba highway on the northern slope of Wadi al-Mujib. This is rather inhospitable country, but stunningly beautiful, so we didn't venture of the main road to search for this one.

DIBON

Allotted to Gad and later to Reuben (Num 32:3; Jos 13:9,17)
'a wasting away'
Also called Dibon-Gad (Num 33:45) and Dimon (Is 15:9). This is where the famous Mesha Stele was found in 1868. There is also a Dibon in southern Judah near the boundary of Edom (see Dibon entry in Negev section).
Num 21:30   Captured by the Israelites
Num 32:34   The children of Gad built Dibon
Jer 48:18,22   Denounced by the prophets

» Dibon is located east of the Jordan River, 5 km north of the River Arnon and now identified with modern Dhiban about 50 km north of Karak on the King's Highway. As you are leaving the northern end of the modern town you will see a signpost to Barza, turning very sharp left. Follow this road for 0.4 km to the ruins.

MACHAERUS

The remains of one of the fortresses of Herod the Great. According to the Jewish historian Josephus Flavius, this is where John the Baptist was imprisoned and beheaded.
Mt 14:3   John the Baptist imprisoned
             Also: Mk 6:17; Lk 3:19,20
Mt 14:6-11   Salome danced and John the Baptist was
             beheaded. Also: Mk 6:21-28

» Beside the village of Mukawir about 50 km from Medeba and overlooking the Dead Sea

MEDEBA

'waters of quiet'
The oldest surviving map of the Bible lands is preserved on the
floor of a sixth century church in Medeba - the Greek Orthodox
St. George's church.

1 Chr 19:7	Ammonites camped before the battle with David
Num 21:30	The Amorites defeated as far as Medeba

» Also called Madaba, this is on the King's Highway about 24 km
southwest of Amman.

PISGAH

'cleft' or 'division'
(Map 27). That part of the Abarim range of mountains near the
northeastern end of the Dead Sea. Its summit is Mt. Nebo, or
Naba. Pisgah is a promontory on the range about 792m above
the Dead Sea. Today it has a church as a memorial to Moses
and a serpentine cross, and is traditionally associated with the
death of Moses. On a clear day the towers of buildings on the
Mt. of Olives can be clearly seen. Nearby is the higher peak
associated with the story of Balak.

Num 22-24	Balaam here many times
Num 23:13-14	Balaam's second oracle for Balak
Deut 3:27;34:1-4	Moses viewed the promised land

» It is about 1 km west of the summit Mt. Nebo and about 8 km west
of Medeba. This particular peak is known locally as Siyagha.

MOUNT NEBO

(Map 27). The highest peak on the Abarim range at 848m
above the Dead Sea.

Num 33:47	Children of Israel encamped nearby
Deut 32:48-52	Moses died on this mountain
Deut 34:1-4	Moses viewed the promised land
Deut 34:5-8	Moses buried in a nearby valley

NEBO

Settled and rebuilt by Reubenites (Num 32:3-38; 1 Chr 5:8)
'elevation'
(Map 27). The village of Nebo (Khirbet el-Mukhayyat), was located on the southern peak of the mountain, 790m above sea level. There was another Nebo near Bethel and Ai (Ezra 2:29); Nehemiah calls it "the other Nebo" (Neh 7:33)

Is 15:2-4   Lamentations in the streets
Jer 48:1-3   Nebo will be ruined

»There is absolutely no local help to aid your search for this one - the 'guides' at Pisgah don't seem to know of its whereabouts, even though it is only 4.5 km away and three churches and a small monastery have been excavated. So, follow map 27.

HESHBON

Populated by Reuben (Jos 13:17) and Gad (1 Chr 6:81)
'stronghold'
(Map 28). Todays village of Hisban covers the southeastern and southern slopes of the Tel.

Num 21:21-30   Sihon, king of the Amorites, refused Israel
                             passage
Num 21:24   Sihon, king of the Amorites, killed
Num 21:25   Israel dwelt in Heshbon
Num 32:1-5   Reuben and Gad requested Heshbon for a
                             possession
Num 32:37   Children of Reuben built Heshbon
Deut 2:30   Sihon, king of the Amorites, refused Israel
                             passage
Deut 3:2   Sihon, king of the Amorites, lived here
Jos 12:1-2   Captured by the Israelites
Jos 13:8-10   The former capital of Sihon, king of the
                             Amorites
Is 15:4   Captured by Mesha, King of Moab
Is 16:8,9   Denounced by the prophets

» Tel Hesban is situated approximately 23 km southwest of Amman and 13 km north of Medeba. Drive north on route #31 from Medeba.

Immediately after passing through the village of Hisban, turn left and follow map 28.

AMMON

The land of Ammon was settled by the descendants of Lot's son (Gen 19:38). It's capital city was Rabbah (Deut 3:11) which is today's city of Amman, Jordan.

Judg 11:28-33   Jephthah devastated the towns of Ammon
Amos 1:13   The Lord's judgment on Ammon

RABBAH

'great'

Today's Amman, the capital city of Jordan. Sometimes called Rabbah-Ammon, in Greek times it was known as Philadelphia and was one of the cities of the Decapolis.

Deut 3:11   The bed of Og king of Bashon in Rabbah
2 Sam 11:1,16,17 Uriah the Hittite killed
2 Sam 12:26-28 Joab defeated Rabbah at the citadel
2 Sam 12:29-31 David captured and plundered Rabbah
1 Chr 20:1   Joab left the city in ruins
Ezk 25:5   Destruction of Rabbah foretold
Amos 1:14   The Lord's judgment on Rabbah

PLAINS OF MOAB

"Do not let this Book of the Law depart from your mouth;
meditate on it day and night, so that you may
be careful to do everything written in it.
Then you will be prosperous and successful.
Have I not commanded you? Be strong and
courageous. Do not be terrified; do not be
discouraged, for the LORD your God will
be with you wherever you go' (Jos 1:8,9)

The flat area east of the Jordan across from Jericho.
Num 22:1   Children of Israel encampment
Num 26:1-4   The second census of the Children of Israel

SHITTIM
'acacia grove'
Also called Abel-Shittim (Num 33:49)

Num 25:1	Men indulged in sexual immorality with Moabite women
Num 25:9	A plague killed 24,000 Israelites
Num 26:2	Moses took a military census of Israelites
Num 27:12-23	Joshua proclaimed as Moses' successor
Num 33:49	Israel camped before entering the land
Jos 2:1	Joshua sent two spies to Jericho
Jos 3:1	Israel camped before entering the land

» The exact location is uncertain but most scholars identify it with Tell el-Hamman; others with the nearby Tell el-Kefrein. Both Tels are on the Plains of Moab somewhere to the east of the Allenby/Hussein Bridge, but we could find neither of them.

GILEAD
'mound of stones'
It is not easy to determine exactly the boundaries of Gilead. In some cases it seems to have been used in a restricted sense, and in some cases in a much broader sense. The name is often applied to general region east of the Jordan River which was allotted to the tribes of Reuben, Gad and the half tribe of Manasseh (Num 32:1-30; Jos 17:1). Today, this would extend approximately from the Arnon River gorge in the south to the Yarmouk River in the north. To the north of Gilead would be the region of Bashan. However, from Deut 34:1 and 2 Ki 10:33, the region of Bashan may have been included in Gilead. There was also a mountain with this name (Judg 7:3; Song 4:1).

Gen 31:21-25	Laban overtook Jacob
Gen 37:25	Exported spices, balm and myrrh
Num 32:1	Famous for its cattle
Judg 11:1	Jephthah the judge was a Gileadite
2 Sam 17:16-26	David fled during Absalom's rebellion
2 Sam 18:9	Absalom's mule
1 King 17:1	Elijah the Tishbite was a native of Gilead

2 King 10:32 32	Hazael, king of Syria victorious
2 King 15:29	Tiglath-Pileser took Gilead captive
1 Chr 5:9	Famous for its cattle
1 Chr 5:10	Reubenites expelled the Hagarites
1 Chr 5:18	Hagarites expelled from the region
Jer 8:22	Is there no balm in Gilead?

ADAM

'red, ground'
(Map 29). Also Adamah (1 Ki 7:46). A city located beside Zaretan (Jos 3:16).
Jos 3:14-17   The people crossed the Jordan, the waters divided, and backed up to Adam

» *Identified with Tel Damiya about 4 km east of the River Jordan, near the junction with the River Jabbok, and 25 km north of the Allenby Bridge. Drive 15.7 km north of Karameh on route #45. Turn west and drive 4.7 km to an army check point. Talk nicely, very nicely, to the officers and the Tel is 0.2 km further on the south side of the road.*

SUCCOTH

In Gad (Jos 13:27)
'booths'
(Map 29). Tel Deir Alla is one of the prominent mounds of the Jordan valley. Some scholars prefer to identify Succoth with Tel el-Ahsas, 2.5 km west of Deir Alla. Another place with this name was the district where the people of Israel first camped after leaving Rameses in Egypt (Ex. 12:37). A few authors identify Deir Alla as Penuel where Jacob wrestled with God (Gen 32:25-32).

Gen 33:17	Jacob lived before reentering Canaan
Jos 13:27	Part of the land to be possessed
Judg 8:4-8	People of Succoth refused to supply Gideon's army
Judg 8:13-16	Gideon punished the men of the town
1 Ki 7:46	Many temple vessels cast here
2 Chr 4:17	Many temple vessels cast here

Ps 60:6   "I will measure off the valley of Succoth"
Ps 108:7   "I will measure off the valley of Succoth"

» Tel Deir Alla is located about 14 km east of the River Jordan near where the River Jabbok emerges from the hills. The Tel is at the northern end of the town of Deir Alla right on the western edge of the road.

RIVER JABBOK

One of the main eastern tributaries of the River Jordan.

Gen 32:22-32   Jacob wrestled with the angel
Num 21:24   Northern boundary of the Ammonites
Deut 3:16   Border of the Ammonites
Jos 12:2   Northern boundary of the Amorites

» The Jabbok arises near Amman and enters the Jordan about 25 kilometers north of the Dead Sea. It crosses route #45 close by Tel Deir Alla, Biblical Succoth.

PENUEL

Jacob called the place Penuel, "For I have seen God face to face" (Gen 32:30). Also called Peniel (Gen 32:30).

Gen 32:22-32   Jacob wrestled with the angel
Gen 32:25   Jacob had his thigh put out of joint
Gen 32:28   Jacob had his name changed to Israel
Judg 8:4-9   People refused to supply Gideon's army
Judg 8:17   Gideon pulled down the tower of Peniel
Judg 8:17   Gideon killed the men of the town
1 Ki 12:25   Jeroboam built up Peniel

» The location of Penuel is uncertain but it is probably on the banks of the River Jabbok not far to the east of Succoth (Judg 8:4-9), perhaps no more than 10 km; a good case is made for a double-hill called Talul ed-Dahab 6 km east of Succoth. Some authors actually identify it as being at Deir Alla. The best location to get a general view of the Jabbok is south of Jaresh. Drive south from Jaresh about 4 km and the first main valley is the Jabbok.

CHERITH BROOK
'gorge, trench'
(Map 30). Most authorities identify Cherith as Wadi Yabis, east of the River Jordan about 12 km south of Beth Shean. Some identify it as the Wadi Kelt west of Jericho.
1 Ki 17:3-6   Elijah fed by ravens
» Traveling north along the Jordan valley road (route #45), drive to the extreme north end of the town of Wadi Yabis. Turn right on to a narrow, but paved road. Cross a constructed water channel, and drive a further 0.6 km on an unpaved track to a right angle turn to the left. From here drive about 100m to the edge of the wadi.

DECAPOLIS
'ten cities'
A district of northern Palestine embracing ten cities - Canatha, Damascus, Dion, Gadara, Gerasa (Jaresh), Hippos, Pella, Philadelphia (Old Testament Rabbah and present-day Amman), Raphana, and Scythopolis (Beth Shean). Only Scythopolis was west of the River Jordan.
Mt 4:25   People followed Jesus
Mk 5:20   Demon-possessed man proclaimed Jesus
Mk 7:31   Jesus preached in this region

GADARENES
Also called Gergesenes and Gerasenes. The identity of these is a little confusing and seems to include Gadara and Jaresh (entries below) and Kursi on the eastern shore of the Sea of Galilee (see Gadara in the Galilee section).

GADARA
'walls'
Gadara was one of the cities of the Decapolis and was the capital city of the Roman province of Perea. The extensive ruins overlook the River Yarmouk, Hamat Gadar, and the Sea of Galilee to the northwest. Refer to Gadara entry in the Galilee section.

Mt 8:28-34   Demon-possessed men healed by Jesus
                   See also: Mk 5:1-20; Lk 8:26-39

» Today's village of Umm Qeis 518m above sea level in the northwest corner of Jordan about 30 km from Irbid.

JARESH

This is possibly Biblical Gerasa. One of the ten cities of the Decapolis, Gerasa is not mentioned by name in the Bible, but it may be inferred from the use of Gerasenes in Mk 5:1 and Lk 8:26,37.

» Jaresh is one of the major archeological sites in the world and is 48 km north of Amman.

SYRIA

RIVER EUPHRATES

At 2900 km long, the Euphrates is the longest river of Western Asia and, along with the Tigris, the two major rivers in Mesopotamia. Its source is in eastern Turkey, it flows through Syria and Iraq, and finally joins the Tigris River before entering the Persian Gulf. In the Bible the Euphrates is referred to as "the Euphrates" (Gen 2:14; 2 Chr 35:20), "the River Euphrates," (2 Sam 8:3) "the great river, the River Euphrates," (Gen 15:18; Jos 1:4), or as "the River" (Deut 11:24; Jos 24:3). God took Abraham "from the other side of the flood (KJV) or "from the land beyond the river" (Jos 24:3) and brought him to the land of Canaan. Jos 24:15 states that the fathers of Israel lived on "the other side of the flood" (KJV) or "beyond the river" (NIV), referring to the Euphrates.

Gen 2:14	One of four rivers from the Garden of Eden
Gen 15:18	Boundary of the lands promised to Israel
Ex 23:31	The eastern limit of the kingdom of Israel
Deut 1:7	The eastern limit of the kingdom of Israel
Deut 11:24	Boundary of the lands promised to Israel
Jos 1:4	Boundary of the lands promised to Israel
2 Sam 8:3	David recovered territory at the Euphrates
1 Chr 5:9	The eastern limit of the kingdom of Israel
2 Chr 35:20	The great battle at Carchemish
Jer 13:1-7	Jeremiah symbolically buries his sash
Jer 51:59-64	Prophecies against Babylon
Rev 9:14	Four angels bound at the Euphrates
Rev 16:12	The river will be dried up

TADMOR - PALMYRA

'palm tree'

Tadmor was known to the Greeks and Romans, and it is known today, as Palmyra. This was the northeastern boundary of Solomon's empire. Tadmor is one of the most impressive archeological sites in the middle east.

1 Ki 9:18	The city is in an oasis in the wilderness
2 Chr 8:4	Solomon built Tadmor in the wilderness

» A city about 200 km northeast of Damascus.

DAMASCUS

Damascus features prominently in one major story from Acts 9:2-25; 22:5-16 where we read of the conversion of Saul of Tarsus, who became Paul, apostle, preacher, and writer of 15 books of the New Testament. The three sites listed are all within the Old City of Damascus, surrounded by a wall which mostly dates to the 13th century. The wall has eight gates (Bab; plural Abwab), and only the restored Bab Sharqi, meaning East Gate, dates back to Roman times. Just outside of the city walls, and to the north, is the River Barada (not a very pleasant 'river') which is the ancient River Abana referred to by Naaman (2 Ki 5:12).

House of Ananias
Acts 9:9   Ananias had a vision
» The entrance to the chapel of Ananias is just inside the city wall midway between Bab Sharqi and Bab Touma. From Bab Sharqi take the first lane on the right and follow it for about 250m to its end.

Straight Street
Darb el-Mustaqim in Arabic, Straight Street is probably so named because it is about the only straight street in an otherwise labyrinthine twisted jumble of alleys and chaotic markets that make up the Old City. There is no tradition linked with the location of the house of Judas.
Acts 9:10   Ananias told to go to the house of Judas
» The street starts at Bab Sharqi and runs for over 1 km through the Christian quarter, passing a Roman arch and eventually becoming Madhat Pasha Souq.

City Wall
Acts 9:25   Paul lowered over the city wall at night
» St. Paul's chapel is built into one of the city gates, Bab Kisan. The chapel can only be entered from inside the city wall. To the left of the gate is a driveway to the new convent. Walk up the driveway and the entrance to the chapel is on your right.

Tomb of John the Baptist, and the Temple of Rimmon
The Omayyad mosque is believed to cover the site of the temple of Rimmon. In the main sanctuary of the mosque is a structure surrounding what the Muslims revere as the tomb of John the Baptist (the prophet Yahia to the Muslims). It is believed that his head was buried here.

2 Ki 5:18   Naaman asks for forgiveness for bowing to
                   Rimmon

» Omayyad Mosque, built in the 8th century AD, is inside the Old City of Damascus at the eastern end of the huge Souq al-Hamadiyyeh. It is a massive and magnificent structure renowned for its multicolored mosaics of trees and landscapes.

RIVER ABANAH

'story'
The main river of Damascus, along with the Pharpar. The Abanah flowed through the center of the city. Also spelled Abana (KJV, NIV).

2 Ki 5:12   A river of Damascus
2 Ki 5:12   Naaman would rather bathe in the Abanah

» It is probably the river known today as the Barada, a short river arising about 30 km to the northwest of Damascus and ending in Lake Bahret Hijaneh about 30 km to the east.

RIVER PHARPAR

'swift'
2 Ki 5:12   A river of Damascus
2 Ki 5:12   Naaman would rather bathe in the Pharpar

» Probably today's River Awaj. It arises in the Hermon range and flows about 15 km south of Damascus. It is a tributary of the River Abanah.

KAUKAB

Since Crusader times, this village has been regarded as the traditional site of the conversion of Saul of Tarsus, to become Paul the apostle; other locations were accepted before this.

Acts 9:1-19   Paul's conversion
Acts 22:4-11   Paul's speech in Jerusalem
Acts 26:12-18   Paul's defense before Agrippa

» Acts 9:3 and 22:6 tell us that Paul's conversion happened "near Damascus" and unfortunately we have no more information to go on. Just below the village of Kaukab, 15 km southwest of Damascus on the road to Quneitra, in the open fields is a small rotunda church marking the traditional site.

UGARIT

Ugarit is not mentioned in the Bible, but it has strong Biblical importance because of the archaeological discoveries made at the site. Ugarit was an important city between the time of Abraham and David (1800 to 1000 B. C.). The most important discovery was a library containing a large number of clay tablets written in many ancient Near Eastern languages. The language is similar to Biblical Hebrew.

» Ugarit is modern Ras Shamra. It was an ancient Canaanite city in northern Syria situated about 40 km southwest of Antioch

CARCHEMISH

'city of Chemosh'
A city beside the Euphrates River (2 Chr. 35:20; Is. 10:9; Jer. 46:2). Carchemish was the ancient capital of the Hittites. In 605BC, Carchemish was the site of one of the most important battles of ancient history when Pharaoh Necho of Egypt and Nebuchadnezzar II of Babylon fought; the Egyptians were defeated.

2 Chr 35:20   Necho king of Egypt fought at Carchemish
Is 10:5-9   God's judgment on Assyria
Jer 46:2   Necho was defeated at Carchemish

» Today's city of Jerablus.

MAPS

MAP 1

OLD CITY, JERUSALEM

1. New gate
2. Damascus gate
3. Zedekiah's quarries
4. Herod's gate
5. Stephen's gate
6. Pool of Bethesda
7. Ecce Homo Convent and Praetorium
8. Ecce Homo Arch
9. Prison of Christ
10. Zalatimo's sweets
11. St. Alexander's Church
12. Church of the Holy Sepulchre
13. Jaffa gate
14. David's citadel
15. Church of St. James
16. Zion gate
17. Convent of the Olive Tree and House of St. Annas
18. Church of St. Mark
19. Middle gate
20. Broad Wall
21. Treasures of the Temple
22. Western Wall
23. Dung Gate
24. El Aksa Mosque
25. Dome of the Rock

OLD CITY, JERUSALEM

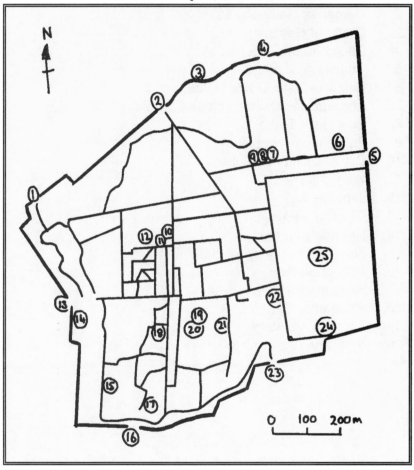

MAP 2

CITY OF DAVID AND THE KEDRON VALLEY

1. Church of Mary Magdalene
2. Garden of Gethsemane
3. Grotto of Gethsemane
4. Church of the Assumption
5. Church of St. Stephen
6. Beautiful Gate; Golden Gate
7. Absalom's Pillar and Tomb of Jehoshaphat
8. Bnei Hezir Tomb
9. Zechariah's Monument
10. City of David excavations
11. Warren's shaft
12. Jebusite wall
13. Gihon Spring
14. Hezekiah's tunnel
15. Tombs of the Kings of Judah?
16. Pool of Siloam
17. Hinnom valley
18. Akeldama
19. Tomb of Annas the High Priest
20. En Rogel

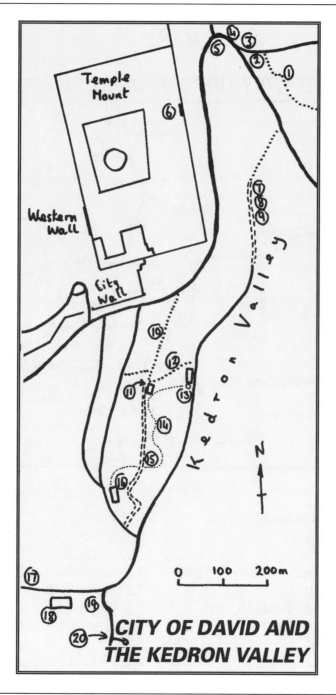

Temple Mount

Western Wall

City Wall

Kedron Valley

N

0   100   200m

CITY OF DAVID AND THE KEDRON VALLEY

MAP 3

TO THE NORTH OF JERUSALEM

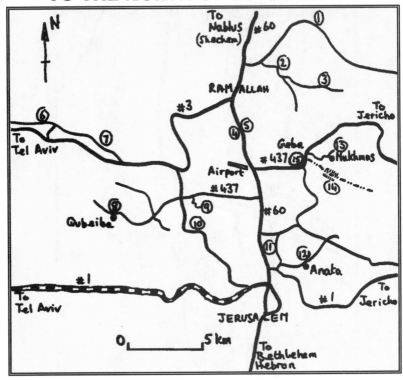

1. Baal Hazor
2. Bethel
3. Ai, Et-Tell
4. Mizpeh,Tel en-Nasbeh
5. Al Bireh
6. Lower Beth Horon
7. Upper Beth Horon
8. Emmaus
9. Gibeon
10. Ramah
11. Gibeah, Tel El Ful
12. Anathoth
13. Michmash
14. 'Jonathan's Gorge'

MAP 4

GIBEON-EL JIB

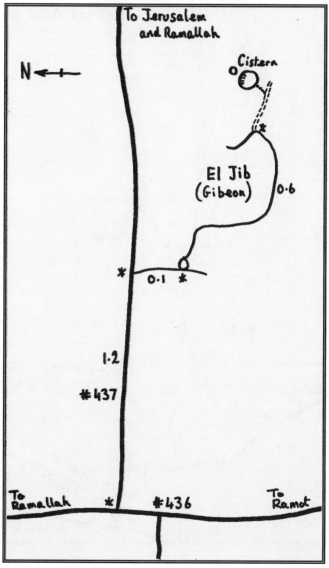

MAP 5

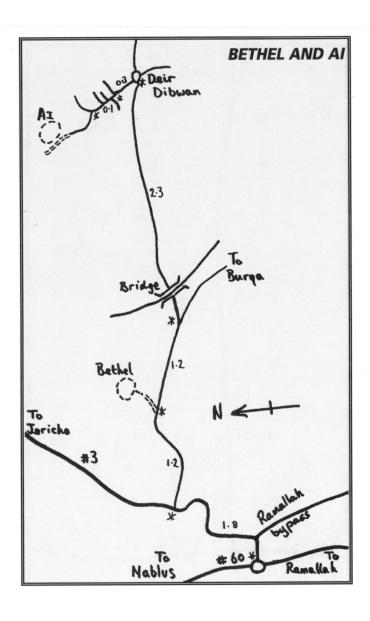

BETHEL AND AI

Arise, walk through the land

MAP 6

NORTHEAST OF RAMALLAH

1. Bethel
2. Ai, Et-Tel
3. Ophrah
4. Baal Shalisha
5. Baal hazor

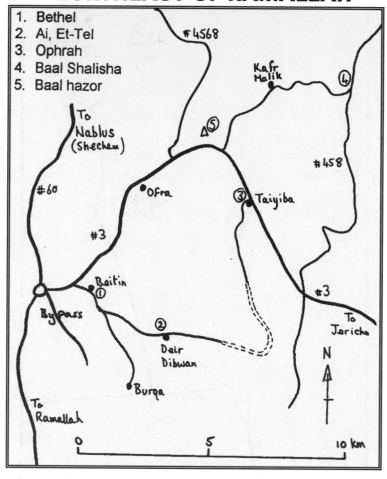

MAP 7

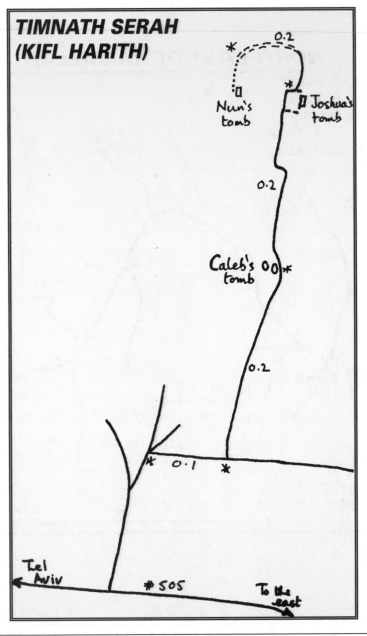

Arise, walk through the land

MAP 8

SHECHEM AND SYKAR

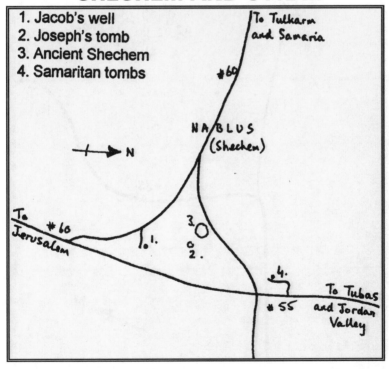

1. Jacob's well
2. Joseph's tomb
3. Ancient Shechem
4. Samaritan tombs

MAP 9

KEILAH

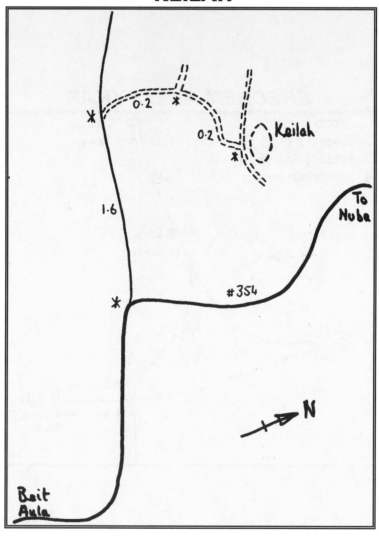

Arise, walk through the land

MAP 10

CARMEL AND MAON

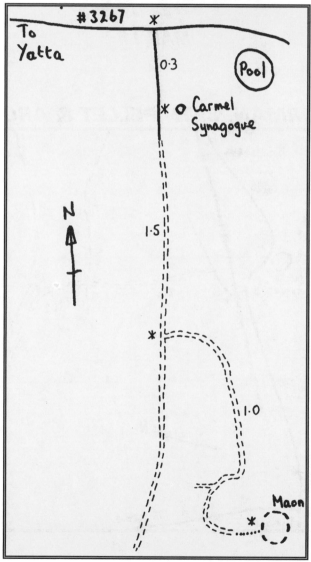

MAP 11

HORMAN, BETH PELLET & AROER

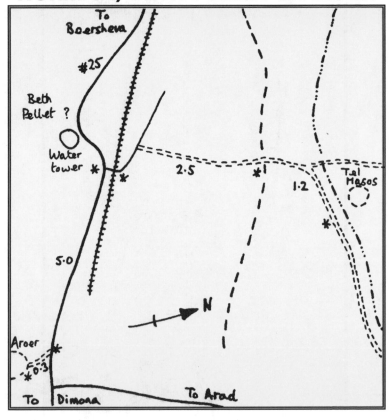

MAP 12

HEROD'S PALACE IN JERICHO

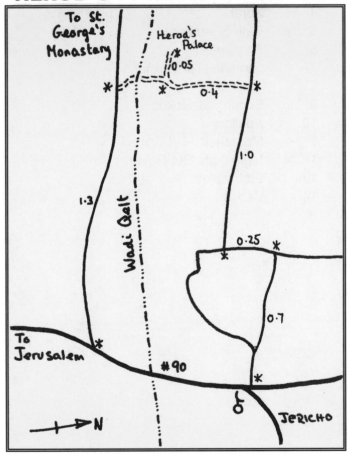

MAP 13

WEST AND SOUTHWEST OF JERUSALEM

1. Gath, Tel Tzafit
2. Ekron, Tel Miqne
3. Timnah, Tel Batash
4. Zorah
5. Beth Shemesh
6. Beit Jimal
7. Jarmuth, Tel Yarmut
8. Azekah
9. Socoh, Tel Sokho
10. Adullam
11. Moresheth, Tel Goded
12. Mareshah, Bet Guvrin
13. Elah valley
14. Lachish

WEST AND SOUTHWEST
OF JERUSALEM

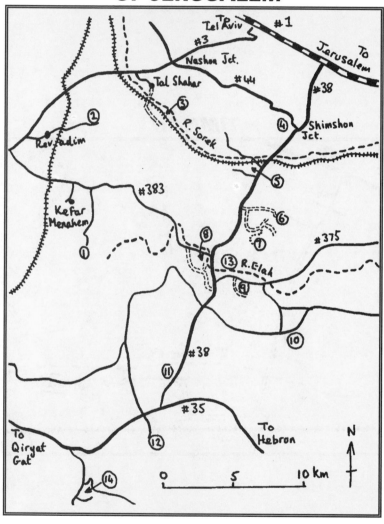

MAP 14

TIMNAH

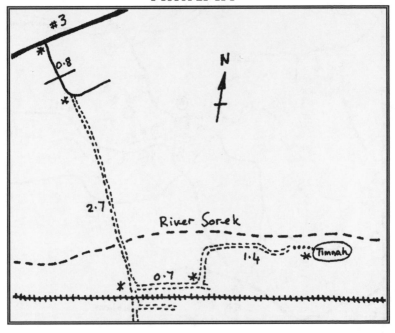

Arise, walk through the land

MAP 15

AIJALON

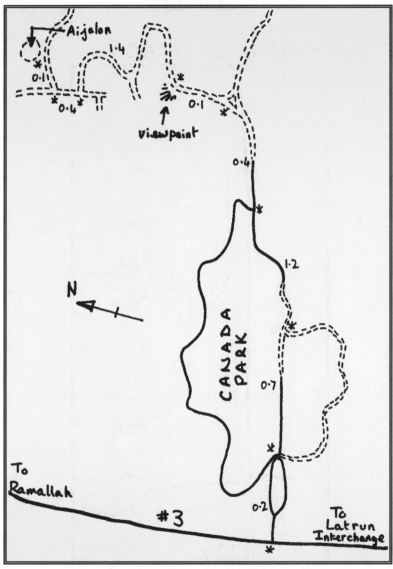

MAP 16

ALTAR OF MANOAH

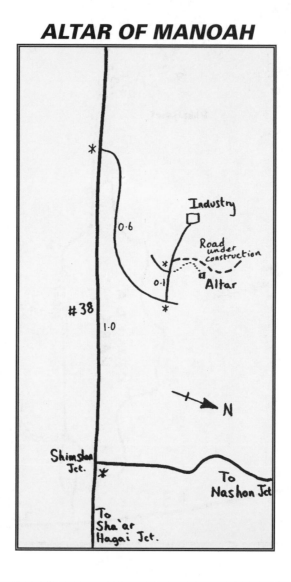

MAP 17

JARMUTH

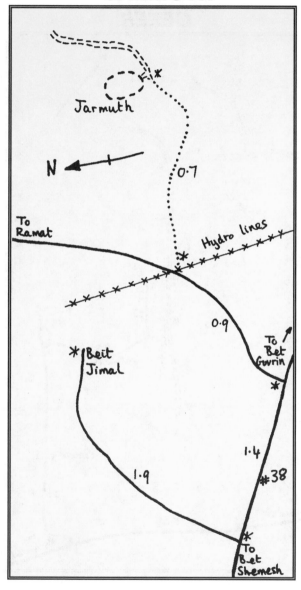

Jarmuth

N

0.7

To Ramat

Hydro lines

0.9

To Bet Guvrin

*Beit Jimal

1.4

1.9

#38

To Bet Shemesh

MAP 18

GEZER

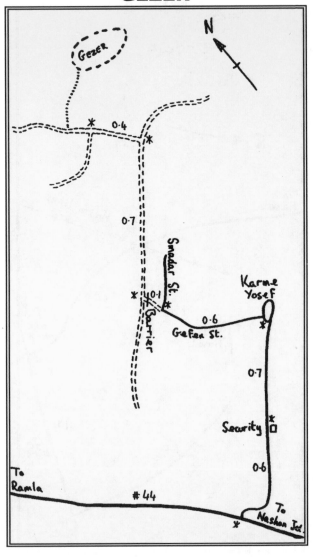

Arise, walk through the land

MAP 19

EGLON

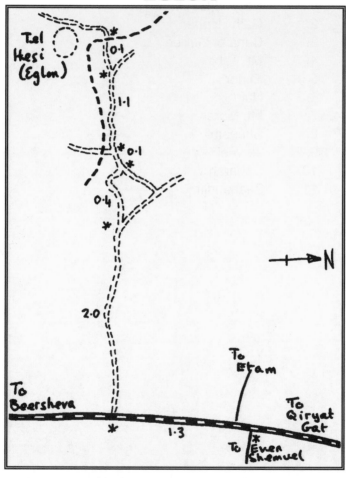

MAP 20

ARMAGEDDON AND TO THE NORTHEAST

1. Sepphoris
2. Gath Hepher
3. Cana of Galilee
4. Mt. Tabor
5. Endor
6. Nain
7. Mt. Moreh
8. Shunem
9. Jezreel
10. Dabarah
11. Zaanannim

ARMAGEDDON AND TO THE NORTHEAST

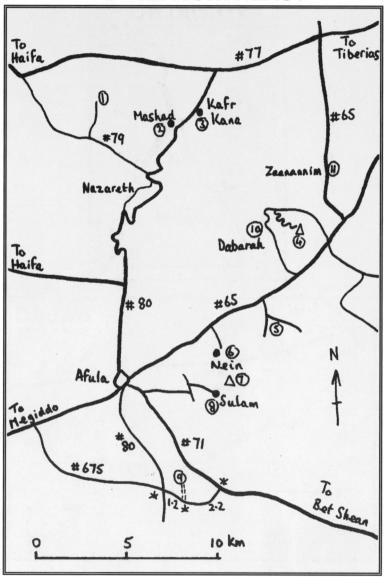

MAP 21

TO ZIKLAG

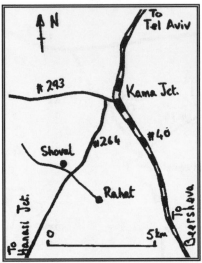

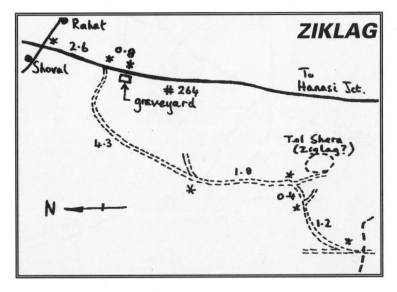

Arise, walk through the land

MAP 22

AFULA(OPHRAH)

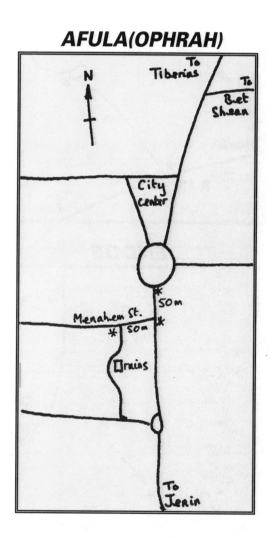

MAP 23

NAIN

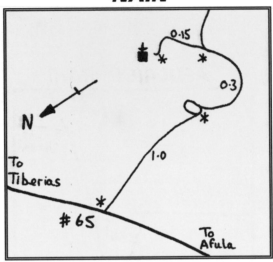

ENDOR

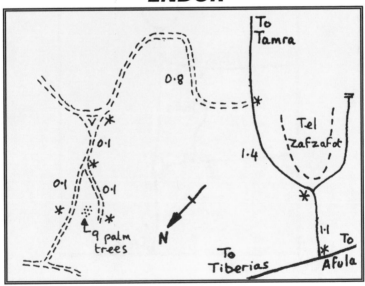

Arise, walk through the land

MAP 24

CANA OF GALILEE

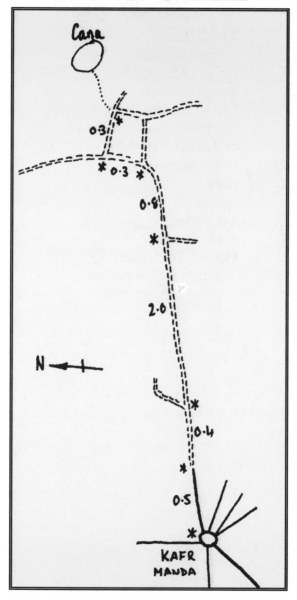

MAP 25

GALILEE

1. Migdal, Magdala
2. Mount of Beatitudes
3. Tabgha
   * Church of the Multiplication
     of the Loaves and Fishes
   * Church of St. Peter
4. Capernaum
5. Korazim
6. Bethsaida
7. Tel Hadar
8. Kursi, Gadara?
9. Hippos, Tel Susita
10. Joseph's well, Ammi'ad

Arise, walk through the land

GALILEE

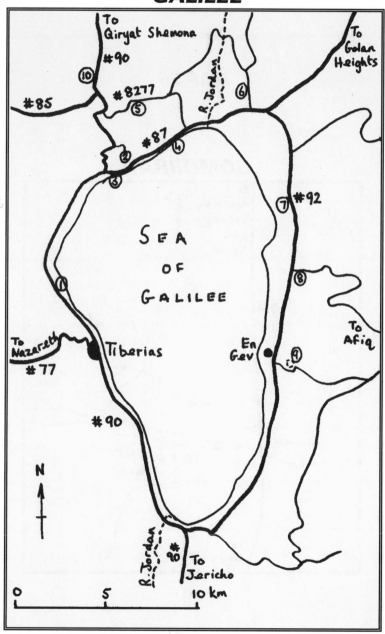

MAP 26

GOMORRAH

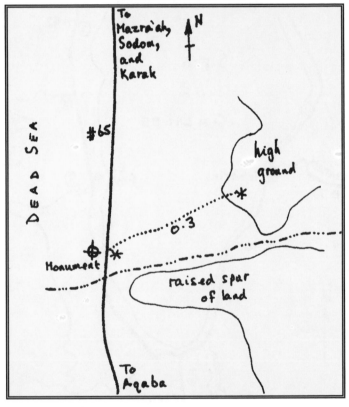

Arise, walk through the land

MAP 27

NEVO AND PISGAH

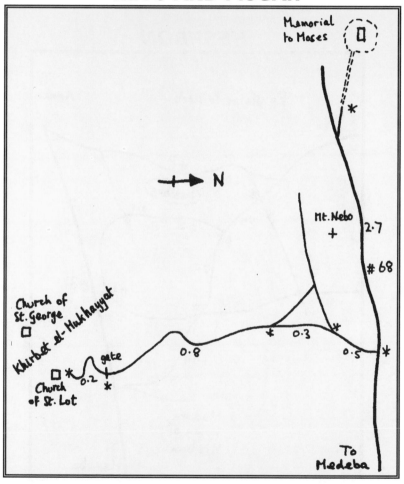

MAP 28

HESHBON

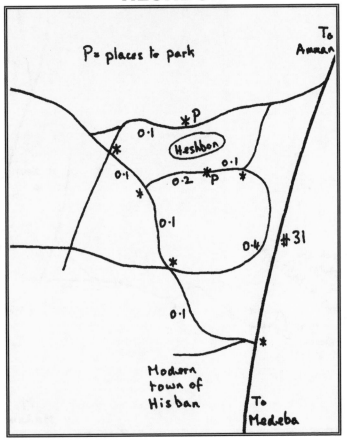

MAP 29

SUCCOTH (DEIR ALLA)
AND ADAM

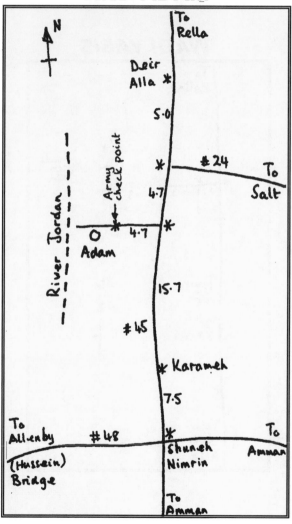

MAP 30

WADI YABIS

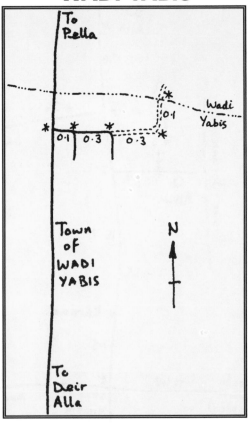

Arise, walk through the land

INDEX

A

Arise, walk through the land

C

D

Arise, walk through the land

Index

Arise, walk through the land

Arise, walk through the land

Arise, walk through the land

Arise, walk through the land

Many travelers to the Holy Land are restricted to a predetermined tour schedule and tend to visit sites marked by impressive churches or ancient ruins. Few people visiting the Holy Land consider the more obscure Biblical sites as places of interest to visit. Yet, many places throughout the region can offer the visitor food for thought, meditation, and inspiration. Many of these towns and villages are off the beaten tourist track, nevertheless, they witnessed some of the most inspiring stories of the Old and New Testaments. There is a tremendous sense of history all around. Every hill and valley, town and village, seems to have some claim to fame. Bible stories take on a whole new dimension as they become real historical events that involved real people. It is exhilarating to follow the footsteps of Abraham, Moses, Joshua, and David, to sit where Solomon was crowned king, and to walk where Jesus walked. This book provides detailed directions and maps to guide you to the vast majority of the sites of the Holy Land, and when you get there, it tells you about all of the Biblical events that occurred.

Roy Turkington was born in Northern Ireland. He has a degree in Biological and Environmental Studies from the New University of Ulster, and completed his doctorate at the University College of North Wales. Roy is a Professor of Botany at the University of British Columbia, Vancouver. He has published more than 80 scientific papers and book chapters in his specialty area of plant ecology. Since 1990 he has made many research-related trips to the Negev desert, and in 1992-93, Roy and his family lived in Jerusalem. Along with his wife Evelyn, he has devoted many years to working with children through the Awana program. Roy and Evelyn have two children, Alistair and Andrea.

Notes:

Notes:

Notes:

Notes: